Silenced By Darkness

by

Kathy Miller

Instant Publisher
Collierville, TN
Instantpublisher.com

ISBN: 978-1-60458-313-7

Subject: Biography

This book is a resource for personal life
in the subject areas of fear/depression.

Edited by Craig Sands

Printed in the United States of America.

Reviews

"As the wife of a minister, mother, and Christian performing artist, life was a stage for Kathy Miller. A stage upon which she had learned to perform with excellence, until the lights went down and the stage curtain closed. The darkness that enveloped her personal thought life and the secrets by which she was bound managed to almost strangle the life out of her. In *Silenced by Darkness*, the secret journey by which she has overcome those controlling fears is revealed.

Every woman, whether single, married with children, grandmother, widow, divorced, believer or nonbeliever has a stage. A stage filled with demands, fears and expectations. *Silenced by Darkness* is a **must read** for those who are searching for freedom and peace of mind! And who in today's society doesn't long for that?"

Karen Hardy Fisk, Women's Ministry Speaker and Concert Artist

"There are people who want you to think they know what they are talking about. For sure, when Kathy Miller shares her personal encounter with the Living God, she knows what she is talking about. Her story of pain and personal struggle will bless and encourage you and will give you a fresh insight into the sovereignty and sufficiency of our God. Out God is real and He is relevant and this book is proof."

Stephen Walley, Founder and Director, Servants Alive Ministries

"Kathy Miller is a picture of perseverance. She would be quick to tell you that it is the grace of God, which has sustained her through the years. Kathy has had many opportunities to quit, but has kept her eyes on Jesus! Through all the pain, the tears, the dark hours, there has been a deep abiding joy that can only come from the presence of the Lord! Kathy's story will encourage you and challenge you to keep pressing on for the prize that is set before us!"

Bill Britt, Pastor, College Heights Baptist Church, Gallatin, TN
Evangelist/Founder of Compel Outreach International

Preface

The purpose of this book is to encourage others who may have stared into the face of depression and needed an understanding ear. During my experience, I longed to find a book that I could relate to, particularly in the realm of vocational ministry. At that time, there was none. Now, for you, there is.

My prayer is that through the pages of this book, you will find that you are not alone and that you can and will make it through your situation. May you be blessed by the hope of knowing that God loves you and has not forgotten you. He longs to restore your joy, so do whatever it takes, my friend, to allow Him to do so.

Contents

Acknowledgments

I am deeply grateful to many who have walked this journey with me and shared in the victory of my newfound joy in life. To my husband, you have stood by me and grown with me during this journey when many others would have chosen differently. You truly are a picture of God's grace in my life and I will always love you, my friend, throughout all time.

To my friend, "K," who reached out to me when no one else could despite her fear of others knowing her secret.

To my mentor in the faith, Faye Braddock...I know you're in glory but I still long to tell you, "Thank you from the bottom of my heart for showing me how to practically live out my faith and stand on Truth against all Hell itself."

To my children who loved me unconditionally even when they did not understand.

To my mom for always being an example of unwavering faith in the face of difficulty and hard times. I have learned much from you.

And finally, to my daddy who, in spite of not wanting certain things about his life revealed, gave me his blessing to do so. He now sees from the other side and I know is pleased with the outcome.

Most of all, thank you, Lord, for meeting me where I was!

Dedication

I would like to dedicate this book to my family at Crossroads Fellowship. You have encouraged us in so many ways and I thank God for sending each of you to us. God has done so many awesome things that we have together both witnessed and experienced. I look forward to the many wonders yet to be seen and experienced with you and our Creator. God bless each of you for your faithfulness to be His feet and hands in our community and throughout our world. I love you.

Unanswered Questions

Chapter 1

The room was blurry as I opened my eyes to find paramedics over my seemingly lifeless body. I couldn't quite make out what they were saying or who they were talking to.

"Kathy! Kathy!" Each beckon grew louder as they slapped my hands and shook my arms.

"Can you hear me?" I heard one of them say.

I remember thinking, "Why are they here and who are they talking to?"

As I fought to awaken, I sleepily looked around the room. There were the horror-stricken faces of dear friends, some who should not have been there at this hour of the night. I was sure my mind must have been playing tricks on me.

The uniformed men continued their routine of checking vital signs and asking questions. Then, they began to try, though unsuccessfully, to persuade me into going to the hospital.

I refused. Why, I'm not really sure. It was fear, I suppose, combined with some lackadaisical apathy. For whatever reason, I wasn't going.

"We have an 'accidental' overdose," I heard them say as they called in the report. The only thing I could be sure of was that I didn't want to feel any more pain, but the pills had failed me. It seemed that no matter how many I swallowed, the pain would not ease, much less go away.

"What on earth have I done and what will all of this lead to?"

- - - - - - -

It's Monday morning, July 13, 1987. I wish I could begin the day by saying, "The golden sunlight burst through her window awakening her to a beautiful, glorious morning," but I can't. The truth is the night had been a long one. It had been only three nights before that the overdose had occurred; but, it seemed as if each night had merged into one long, fitful nightmare.

Now, during these early morning hours, there was an ever present truth to the old adage that Mondays are blue. As I looked out the window, the rain was beating down on the lake outside Ronni's backyard. It could not begin to compare with the gloom I knew was all too real in my heart. I began handling last minute details...phone calls, confrontations which seemed like final good-byes and packing for the trip which lay before me.

As we made the journey across miles of endless stretch, Ronni, Saundra, Jerry and I tried to laugh and make light of my "new beginning." Inside, however, my heart was not light but heavy from the load it was bearing.

I began to try to piece it all together in my mind. "How had it all happened?" Events had transpired so rapidly, I felt as if my mind was spinning in comparison to the house caught in the middle of the tornado on *The Wizard of Oz*. Now I was sinking into a whirlwind that was much more vivid and real than some television movie.

Only a few days before, I had flown to Texas for the occasion of my best friend's wedding. I was so excited! As Gary and the kids put me on the plane, we kissed, said "I love you," and "see you in a few days." Now, I was on my way to Fort Worth to be admitted as a patient at the Psychiatric Institute. Could all of this even be possible? Is this reality or will I awaken to discover it is all a bad dream?

Upon arrival at the Psychiatric Institute, I was so numb that the only way I knew we were there was that sick feeling in my stomach which quickly alerted me the moment I saw the place. To my surprise and great delight, they did not have room for me; instead, they put me in a building across the street called Medical Plaza.

"Oh, thank you, God!" I cried from within.

"That sounds so much better than Psychiatric Institute!"

At least now someone could send me a card without printing that label across the front of the envelope for all the world to see! After all, how was this going to look? I was the wife of a minister!

That's right. I had been married to a licensed, ordained Baptist minister for almost nine years. We had two beautiful children, ages seven and five. God had just called us to serve on staff at a wonderful spirit-filled church in Jacksonville, Florida; yet, I was about to enter the psychiatric ward of a hospital almost a thousand miles away from home. ***"What's wrong with this picture?!!"*** There was something about all of this mess that just didn't seem to add up, at least in my estimation.

My thoughts became fixed on the family I had left behind. How I ached inside to think of my precious husband without his wife and my dear, sweet children without their mama. How could they possibly continue to love me? Our lives had become a mess simply because I was falling apart. Was this a breakdown? Who was this person housed inside this feeble body, confused and so alone?

As I looked back on my life, I tried to recall the young, innocent little girl sheltered from life's hurts and problems by a loving father. If he could prevent it, she would never have the pain and cares this ugly world has to offer. Back then, she was so full of life, love and joy. The person she had become was now full of fear, loneliness and confusion.

"What could have caused such change in me?"

Then I began to remember. It seemed that so much of my life had been filled with hurt, pain or disappointment. Oh yes, there had been many blessings, too. At this particular moment in time, though, they were locked away, as if being a secret, in some very dimly lit corner of my mind. What was screaming out at me like flashing neon marquees, however, was the reality of the adversities that had come into my life.

No matter how hard someone may try to spare us, we all have them, don't we? They are a part of life. No one is exempt and each person's experience is as important and perhaps life-changing as another's. You can probably count on each difficulty to be very diverse in regards to the circumstances, each being uniquely packaged according to the individual's need for growth.

For instance, mine may be disguised as a beautiful package wrapped in pink paper with a large, fuchsia bow on top, where yours may be wrapped in blue with navy streamers hanging from it. No matter how it may appear on the outside, when unwrapped we find the experience of ...*life!* In that box, along with some very wonderful experiences, there will inevitably be adversity, trials and struggles. And when we find ourselves in such a state, just as I had found myself that fateful day, we would much rather send the gift back for a full refund with a note attached reading, "Some gift!"

As I thought back upon my life, I was sure that I had had my share of disappointments ... and then some more! They had started so long ago. The first major shaking of my "not so firm" foundation had happened almost fourteen years before. I had pushed it so deep within me that I never thought about it any more. It was hard for me to even remember her; but it had really happened. That was a fact. A part of my comfortable world came crashing down and my life unknowingly began to change that very day.

Bunchie

Chapter 2

"Don't contort your face that way," she'd warn.

"It isn't very becoming to a young lady."

Those words came from the lips of my great aunt whom we lovingly called Bunchie. How she adopted such a name, I'm not exactly certain, except to say that's what her younger brother called her and therefore, that's who she became.

Hazel Simpson, Bunchie to us, was my mama's daddy's sister. As you will soon realize, she was my most favorite person in all the world.

"Why?"

I wouldn't truly learn the answer to that question for some time, but somehow, she always made me feel good…about myself, about the world, about everything. You see, she loved me and I knew she loved me. I was very aware that she enjoyed being with me and I dearly cherished every moment I spent with her! I knew I was special to her. She never had to say it; she just had a way about her that would always let me know.

She and Paul, her husband, would take me on special trips to the Smoky Mountains to enjoy the autumn leaves, have picnics by the roadside and look for hungry bears to feed along the way. We'd also go to Cherokee, North Carolina to learn about and see the Indians.

"Are you ready for the day?" she'd ask on Saturdays.

It was then I knew my adventure was about to begin. Bunchie and I would have a day out for just us girls. First, she would take me to the beauty shop. That's what they called it back then, you know. Remember? Oh, I thought that nothing could be grander than all of that extra special pampering; and sitting under that big, warm hair dryer…I can almost go to sleep thinking about how relaxed it could make a vivacious, spirited young girl.

Then, she would let me walk with her to Scarbrough's store and on to visit the local Avon® lady. There I'd be in a world of my own filled with luscious lipsticks (little ones that were just my size…I didn't know they were samples), colorful eye shadows, creamy rouge and heavenly perfumes.

"How do I look?" I'd ask without fail.

"You're the prettiest young lady I've ever seen," her response was always the same.

Now, I know that wasn't necessarily true, because I've seen pictures of me at that age and "Oh, Brother!" But she made me feel as if it was true and in her own eyes, I believe it was true.

From that moment on, I was hooked! A "true blue" girl, through and through, loving lace, frills and pretty things for the rest of my life. To this day, the sight of an Avon® book just draws me to buy like a thirsty horse to water.

Bunchie, herself, always had the most wonderful smell. I know now that it was the scent of Jergen's® lotion. If it hadn't been for Bunchie, Jergen's® lotion just might have gone out of business, as she must have been one of their largest consumers. Even now, the fragrance of Jergen's® lotion is like a perfume from heaven taking me back to a past of warmth, security and an overall sense of being loved.

"What was so special about this woman?"

Probably not much in the world's way of thinking. She was average-looking, wearing cat-eyed glasses which, of course, were very stylish at the time. She worked at the hosiery mill during the week and went to church regularly on Sundays.

That was about it. Nothing earth shattering.

But in my memory, God has never made anyone who could measure up to this woman. In my estimation, she stood above all the rest. More royal than the Queen of England and more saintly than Mother Teresa was she.

Of course, she was human and she did have her flaws. There were times I even saw them for myself, but they didn't really matter to me or influence the way I felt about her at all. She felt the same way about me. I know because she always treated me the same whether I was good or bad, and I knew deep down inside that she just loved me for being me.

To love someone that way ...just because...is the truest form of love known to man handed down to us by God Himself. He instructs us in His Word:

"Love is very patient and kind, never jealous or envious, never boastful or proud, never haughty or selfish or rude. Love does not demand its own way. It is not irritable or touchy. It does not hold grudges and will hardly even notice when others do it wrong. It is never glad about injustice, but rejoices whenever truth wins out. If you love someone, you will be loyal to him no matter what the cost. You will always believe in him, always expect the best of him, and always stand your ground in defending him."

I Corinthians 13:4-7_{TLB}®

Have you ever had to be corrected by someone and later felt like you were really a bad person or thought somehow that you just couldn't quite measure up?

Bunchie never made me feel that way. I'm not really sure how she did it, but when she corrected me (like when I did that funny thing with my face), it never gave me that awful "you've really messed up!" feeling. I always knew her heart and I knew that any correcting was for my own good. Oh, I hated her having to bring it to my attention, but I knew when she did that it was because she loved me. I guess she was the clearest picture of unconditional love I had ever known on this earth.

I don't want to make it sound as if this was the only love I had ever known because I came from a family full of love. I had wonderful loving parents, aunts and uncles with whom I shared close relationships. I also had grandparents on both sides of my family, and even great grandparents, a blessing which most people are not fortunate enough to experience. Bunchie was just very special and there is really no way to put into words how I felt about her.

As I grew into those years of deciding on a career choice, Bunchie was very instrumental in how all of that would turn out. You see, no one in my family had ever gone to college. Not my parents, grandparents, aunts, uncles, cousins...I mean NOONE!

I grew up in a small town in east Tennessee and my daddy had a picture in his mind of colleges taking innocent little girls and turning them into "worldly women" that would send them down a spiral toward corruption. He never intended for me to go. Oh, he did want me to further my education, but his idea of further education was for me to attend a vocational school.

During my search for God's will for my future life, I went to my pastor for wisdom and guidance. We had a very enlightening conversation.

"Brother Charles," that's what we called him.

"Yes, Kathy, come in my dear."

"How do you begin to discern what God is leading you to do with your life?" I've never forgotten his reply.

"This is the best advice I know to offer. Find something you enjoy doing so much that you would do it for nothing; then, do it well enough that someone will be willing to pay you for it. That way, you will always be happy in your life's work and that's how you will know what God has designed for you to do."

That seemed simple enough to me at the time, so I began to apply that advice to fit my personal situation. After much consideration and endless praying, it became very evident to me the direction to which I was being pointed.

The only thing that would really fit into this "formula" that I loved to do was singing. Coming from a musical family, I had been singing all my life, even singing solos in church at a very young age. During my teenage years, however, I had begun taking my singing much more seriously and deeply desired to excel in the talent that had been given to me by my Creator. I enjoyed it more than anything I had ever done in my life. I used to say, "I'd rather sing than eat!" The more I pondered the idea, the more excited I became and finally knew this was the direction to which God was leading. "I can use what I love to do most to glorify God the rest of my life!" I thought.

"How Cool!"

My life was beginning to fall into place like tightly fit pieces in a jigsaw puzzle. Yeah, it made perfect sense to me…but would it make any sense at all to Daddy?

"Houston, we have a problem!"

They didn't teach singing in vocational schools. If this was really going to be my chosen career, college was the only option and I've already told you what my daddy thought about that.

During this time in which I had been battling for answers concerning what my contribution to this life would be, Bunchie had been struggling with a battle of her own …cancer. She fought long and hard but the time came when she was nearing the end. I'm sure she took care of many things during those last days of her life, but she wasn't slack where I was concerned and she certainly did not leave me out of her final plans.

She knew how much I loved to sing. She loved to hear me sing and she wanted me to pursue it as a career. She made a point to speak with my daddy concerning the subject.

"John, Kathy is a very special young lady."

"Yeah. I'm really proud of her."

"You know I love her as if she were my own."

"Yes, I know you do."

"I'm not going to be here to see her grow up. I know my time is short now, so I have one favor to ask of you, if I may."

"You can ask me anything."

"She loves to sing so much and she really needs the opportunity to go to college to further train her voice. Will you please grant her this wish?"

"If that's really what she wants to do, I'll make sure that it happens."

"Thank you, I know you won't be sorry."

If you were to ask my daddy today, he would tell you that the only reason he agreed to allow me to go to college was because he could not refuse Bunchie her dying wish.

On July 19, 1973, I turned seventeen years of age and two days later, Bunchie died.

How do you handle losing someone that meant more to you than words could express? I didn't think any human could ever understand the grief I was experiencing. I felt nothing but deep hurt and emptiness.

"God, why would such a saint of yours be taken from this world when there was so much left for her to do? When I need her so much in *my* life? I don't understand this."

I was angry at the One who held such power in His hands. When it came down to the heart of the matter, I knew He could have prevented her suffering and her dying, so why had He not intervened?

Buckets of tears poured continuously from me and a groan from deep within wanted to come forth wailing but somehow, I managed to quench and silence it.

As I sat alone, brokenheartedly and grieving at the funeral parlor the evening before Bunchie's burial, I overheard a conversation taking place between two women. They were discussing, if you will, my mourning. One of them said to the other:

"Look at that young girl over there."

"Why is she so upset?"

"Wasn't she just her great aunt?"

My heart ached and I wailed from within as I silently screamed, "Oh, if they only knew...if they only knew!"

Life Goes On

Chapter 3

I somehow went through the motions doing all that was expected of a loved one during a memorial service and then this beautiful woman, now a memory of my past, was placed in the ground. One month later, I began my senior year in high school and on May 21, 1974, I adopted the proud title of "high school graduate." A large chapter of my life had closed and a new one was ready for opening but first, an unexpected tragedy lay lurking in the shadows.

The weekend of June 1, my parents had tickets to the Grand Ole Opry and made plans for a weekend getaway with a couple of their friends, Margie and Jackie Sartin. My friend Janice and I stayed at the home of my pastor and his wife, with whom we had become dear friends, while my parents took their weekend getaway. To me, they were like a second set of parents.

I was awakened during the very early morning hours of Sunday by my uncle, Ronnie.

"What's wrong?" were the first words out of my mouth.

"Your house has burned."

"**What?**"

I think I was in a state of shock for the next several minutes and then a myriad of questions began to flood my mind.

"Did Mama and Daddy know?

"Was my brother, Kent, all right?" He was supposed to be staying at the house that night.

"What about my dog, Little Bit?"

Uncle Ronnie assured me that everyone was fine and that Mama and Daddy were on their way home and that they would be there by later morning.

After Uncle Ronnie left, we all went back to bed and tried, at best, for a few hours of restless sleep until morning. That morning, being Sunday, I was scheduled to sing in a trio with my friends, Janice and Sandra. We had just recently begun having two worship services at our church and in the early morning service there was no choir. We were the only special music there would be. But how could I sing, knowing what had just happened to my family?

I knew I had a responsibility, so with lots of prayer support from my pastor and friends, God was faithful and gave me the strength to sing. The words rang out to such a poignant song:

"You ask me why my heart keeps singing?

Why I can sing when things go wrong?

But since I've found the Source of music,

I just can't help it...God gave the song."[1]

I think I began that day to learn and understand the reality of God's grace and unfailing faithfulness in my life. Maybe I would forget it somewhere down the road, but His work in my life had begun.

After church that day, I was taken to my house to witness the devastation. As I looked up, there stood my mama and daddy, heartbroken over the loss of their home.

"Hey, babe." Daddy tried to sound brave.

"Come with me and we'll walk through the house together."

It was an older home, built well and therefore, was still standing, but it was completely gutted. We had lost everything.

As we walked through the front door, the smell of soot and ash was sickening. With each step we'd take, water would gush from the carpet as a result of the battle fought some hours before by the firemen with their hoses.

Over in the corner was the television. It had melted onto the floor as if to say, "I surrender." We continued walking through the living room and made our way slowly up the stairs toward our bedrooms.

I stood in the doorway of my room, my special place of refuge, shocked by the horror of the sight that lay before my eyes.

"My graduation gifts. They're all ruined."

I had only graduated twelve days ago. Talk about growing up in a hurry. It all seemed like a huge nightmare.

I went to my bed and picked up a stuffed animal that had been given to me by a past boyfriend.

"My camel from Alan. His neck is broken."

I walked over to my closet and my eyes landed on one particular item.

"My dress, my beautiful dress!" I began to sob.

It was the formal I had worn to the Teenboard dance and to my senior prom. Mama had told me we didn't have the money to buy it, but I wanted it so much and begged so hard that Daddy found a way to get it. He always did. It had meant so much to me that I could actually wear a dress from a bridal boutique and not a homemade one like I had worn the previous year. "It's completely destroyed."

The plastic that had once covered it for protection was now melted into the fabric itself. My heart was broken and my tattered emotions cried out to the man who had always been my source of security.

"Daddy, what are we going to do?" I said as I fell into his arms.

Embracing me with such love and with tears in his eyes, he replied, "I don't know, baby; I don't know."

"What do you mean you don't know?" my mind screamed.

"You're my daddy, you always know!" I sobbed even harder.

That's the first time in my life that I could remember Daddy not having the answer to my problem or being able to fix what was wrong. It was frightening for me to see my father who represented strength and security become so vulnerable. A startling revelation had just come my way. Standing there before me was a person, a real human being. Daddy was not *Superman,* who, in my fairy-tale world, was thought to have complete control over the affairs of this hurtful life.

During this difficult day, however, while he was searching for answers himself, Daddy took the time to teach me something of great value, which has forever made a lasting impression on me.

"Honey, we lost our house today, but always remember it's not a house that makes a home. A house is just a building where people eat and sleep. A home represents the people who live together and love one another." He continued on, "Houses can be replaced. People cannot. I've been to many fires in my day and have tragically seen loved ones not come out alive."

Daddy had been captain of the Loudon County Rescue Squad for years, so this was not a new experience for him. It was just now that such a tragedy had happened to him and his family personally.

"We're all safe, so we may not have a place to live, but we have our family and *that* is the true meaning of a home." I knew then that somehow, by God's grace, we could and would continue on with our lives. This truth was great comfort to me at such an insecure moment in my life. We did make it through that summer due to the gracious and loving care of God's people. Our church supported us with a huge outpouring of kindness. One family gave us their house to live in while they were away at school for the summer months, and many others gave us money, took us shopping for new clothes and anything else that was necessary to help us start over again.

By fall, we had bought a small house where we could begin again, and I was ready to head to Cookeville, Tennessee where I would begin my studies as a voice major in music education at Tennessee Tech University.

A Family Built

Chapter 4

I was sitting in string class with a cello between my legs trying to figure out how the thing worked when the young man to my right began to strike up a conversation with me.

"I can't believe it!" I thought. I had noticed him before and he was so cute! Now, he eluded to the fact that he might seem just a little bit interested in ME! At least that's what I thought by his flirtatious actions until I realized he was reading a letter from a girl.

"Another one?" is what ran through my mind.

Gary Miller got a letter from a different girl almost every day, or so it seemed to me. I could understand why because just being around him made you feel good. He had an award-winning personality, a great smile, his sense of humor couldn't be beat, and he certainly wasn't bad to look at, as I have previously stated. Actually, he was gorgeous! But, did I want to be just another girl added to his mailing list? No Way!

Any thoughts I might have had of being interested in him, I purposefully dismissed and set myself toward getting a date with his roommate. After all, he was cute and pretty cool, too.

In the process of trying to accomplish that task, I wound up getting to know Gary a lot better because they were always together. They were both voice majors, also. Finally, when it came time to ask someone to escort me to my spring sorority banquet, I decided it was Gary that I really wanted to go with me. I had begun to really like him by now.

I waited until I knew I would see him and just as expected, he came toward me on the front steps of Derryberry Hall.

"Hi Gary, beautiful day, huh?"

"Sure is; feels great out, doesn't it?"

"Yeah."

"On your way to class?"

"Yeah."

Boy was I nervous, so I just took a deep breath and went for it.

"Listen, my sorority is having their spring banquet in a couple of weeks and I was wondering if you would like to go with me?"

Then came the polite brush off. "Well, I'd really like to, if I can. I've been having to work for my dad some on weekends lately, but I'll check with him and then let you know, if that's all right with you?"

"Sure, that would be great!"

"I'll let you know as soon as I can."

"Okay, see you later."

I knew he was just being nice, so all I could do was wait. A few days later, he saw me and told me to my great delight that he didn't have to work for his dad that day and that he could go. It was a date!

I had already fallen head over heels in love with this guy; so after the banquet when he walked me to my dorm and kissed me goodnight under the moonlight, I knew he was the one God had chosen for me. You see, I had been praying my entire life that God would direct me to the man He intended for me to spend my life with. Now, I knew it was Gary Miller. I had no doubts. The man of my dreams finally had a name.

We dated the rest of that quarter and went back to our hometowns to work for the summer. During that time, I stayed "true" to my newfound love, so to speak, but he wasn't quite as ready to be "tied down" to one girl. I even ended up quitting school for awhile because I was miserable being in love with someone who was not yet convinced that I was the one for him.

After I went back to school, we renewed our friendship but not a romantic relationship. We sang in a Christian group together and were best buddies. I never stopped loving him even though I dated someone else for awhile.

Finally, being that patience has never been my strongest suit, and Gary didn't seem to be coming around, I decided to take matters into my own hands. I was sure that God could use my help to speed things along, and I began to help Him all I could. Trust me, that is never a good decision. Just as always, God was getting ready to teach me that from experience.

Without going into detail, let's just say that I began to initiate a life of pretense and manipulation in order to attempt getting this man's attention. Nothing worked. All the scheming, all the planning was totally in vain because I was trying, and with much effort, to accomplish what only God could do.

One Sunday evening as I was sitting in church, I began to pray and sincerely seek God about the matter. I remember saying, "Lord, what's wrong? I know that Gary is the one you've chosen for me, so why aren't things working out?" The answer came loud and clear.

Did I hear God speak to me audibly? No, when God speaks to the heart, it seems even louder than that.

"It's because you are going about everything the wrong way. Why not be completely honest with Gary and then completely trust Me?"

Instantly, I was convicted of my self-sufficiency and lack of trust in God. I surrendered myself wholly and gave it all to Him that night. I knew what I had to do next.

I went to Gary's house that evening and waited for him to make the trip back from Decatur where he directed music for a church on Sundays. When he arrived, he was surprised to find me there.

"Can we talk?" is all I said.

"Sure. Is something wrong?"

"Not really. Please bear with me because this is very hard for me to say. I feel like I need to be honest with you about my feelings for you. Everyone on this entire campus seems to be aware of the fact that I'm in love with you, although you yourself have failed to see it. I'm not asking you for anything and I want you to know that I'm not angry with you about anything, but I can't hang around with you as a 'pal' any longer. It's killing me to spend so much time with you and not be able to have the kind of relationship with you that I so desire."

After his initial shock, he began to speak, "I really don't know what to say. I don't want to hurt you, but I also have to be honest. I wish I could tell you I feel the same way about you, but I don't. I do love you, but I love you like a sister. I'm sorry."

"That's okay," I said. I just want you to understand why I won't be coming around any more."

"I understand and again, I'm sorry," Gary offered.

When I left that evening, I left with a broken heart. I would be lying if I said otherwise; yet in my heart, I knew I had done the right thing. I would just have to trust God to work it all out.

That's the best part. When you finally let God have control and allow Him to do His own work, He gets results you couldn't have got on your own in a million years.

Do you know that Gary Miller asked me out the very next day? He asked me to go to dinner. I casually tried to brush him off saying I didn't have enough money to go out to eat. Then, he said, "I'll buy." The man was asking me out for a "real" date! Our relationship of a very different nature began that day. That was in January of 1978, and by April 18th, he asked me to marry him. He proposed to me by kneeling on one knee on a little covered bridge at a very beautifully secluded spot called Hidden Hollow and on July 22, 1978, we became husband and wife.

When I finally let the Lord have control, everything just fell into place beautifully. Those two years of waiting and frustration taught me that God is faithful to keep His promises, but we must trust Him to bring them about in His way and in His time.

Since God's timing is always perfect, it didn't matter that **we** had thought it best to be married a few years before having children. God chose, instead, to give me the gift of pregnancy when we had only been married five months. I was still adjusting to being away from Mama and Daddy, being the wife of a minister and now, I was going to be a mother.

On our first wedding anniversary, I was as big as a cow and two months later, it happened. I did, indeed, become a mother. Tuesday morning, October 2, 1979, at 8:40 a.m., Julie Adelle Miller made her entrance into this world. She was the most beautiful thing I had ever laid eyes on. I loved her instantly. Something within me had told me she was a girl early on in the pregnancy. Now it was confirmed. I was ready for the joy she was already bringing to our lives.

What did she look like? She had dark hair, a round face, chubby cheeks and the biggest, brightest, most beautiful blue eyes you have ever seen. As she began to grow, she could use those eyes to steal your heart away...she still can! She was very smart and when she began to talk, she spoke in sentences almost from the very beginning. One thing she accomplished rather quickly was potty training. She was completely trained, including nighttime, at age twenty-two months. I didn't realize what a blessing that was at the time; but looking back, that is exactly the month I became pregnant with our second child. Isn't God good to take care of even the smallest details of our lives?

I grew larger and larger with our second child until one day the doctor said, "You're either going to have twins or you're going to deliver three weeks early." Twins do run in my family. On my great grandmother's side, for who Julie is named, there are six sets of twins. My grandmother had a set of twins; so, in order to find out whether or not that was the case, Dr. Chambers ordered an ultrasound. Back then, they had not yet begun to do ultrasounds as part of routine check-ups like they do today, so this was a rather extraordinary and exciting experience for us. The ultrasound was scheduled and Gary accompanied me to the appointment with great anticipation. We discovered that day that I was right on schedule and there were no twins but rather, one big, healthy boy! We were so thrilled to know that we would have a son.

You see, Gary had been adopted by his parents when he was only four hours old. That was in God's designed plan for him and he has never regretted it for one moment. He has wonderful parents! Having a son just seemed to be a special blessing. I was thrilled to know that Gary's bloodline could continue on for another generation.

I went into labor on Saturday, May 8, 1982, while sitting in the stands watching Gary play in a church softball tournament. I knew it was time because I was already six days past my due date and Julie had been exactly six days late.

Gary took me home and helped me get situated, then went back to play ball while I was to lie down and rest. A few minutes later, he walked through the door.

"What are you doing here?"

"I couldn't go back and play ball knowing you were here in labor with our child. What kind of husband would I be?"

I'll have to admit, there had been times in our marriage when I had wondered just how much playing ball meant to him. He's a sports fanatic with a capital "F," but now I really knew. It wasn't all that important to him, after all.

We carefully made our way to the hospital around 6:30 that evening. I was dilated to four centimeters. After awhile, I dilated to five centimeters but things were progressing very slowly. At 12:30 a.m., after hours of hard, fast, never-ending, excruciating labor, I was still only five centimeters.

"I can't have this baby. He's too big!"

"I don't believe he's as big as your last one," said Dr. Chambers.

"I don't care, something's wrong, I can't do it this time!"

"Let's go ahead and break your water, and we'll see what happens from there."

"Fine, just do it. I need some help."

After breaking my water, I had a very hard contraction with the urge to push.

"Gary, I know it's too soon, but I've got to push. Call the nurse."

"What's the matter sweetie?" she asked me.

"I feel like I need to push, but he just broke my water and I know it's too soon."

"All right, hon, we'll just check you to see what's going on." Then she continued: "Oh, my goodness, you're fully dilated. You're ready to deliver this baby, but don't push yet."

"Yeah , right! Easy for you to say!" "Ugghhh…!!"

At this point, she threw a surgical jumpsuit at Gary and said, "Here, put this on, you don't have time for that other one."

Things got pretty hectic at that point. She had the doctor paged and told him what was going on, but his take on the situation was: "I just checked her. She was only dilated to five. She's not ready to deliver that baby."

"She's having this baby." "She's ready!" the nurse tried to persuade.

Gary began to fumble around getting on his jumpsuit and surgical booties as quickly as possible. The orderlies were asking me to pick my bottom up and put it on the gurney which would transfer me to the delivery room. I was hyperventilating and having leg cramps. Somebody help!

To sum it all up, I dilated from five centimeters to ten centimeters and delivered our son in eighteen minutes flat. It was pretty fast and furious.

To the doctor's surprise, Christopher Ryan Miller was born at 12:48 a.m., May 9, 1982, which just happened to be Mother's Day. What a blessed mother I was! He weighed almost nine pounds and looked so different than his sister had. He was very long, had strawberry blonde hair, clear blue eyes and a narrow face. He also had a tiny, tip-shaped nose that looked just like his daddy's and gave me something to tease Gary about.

How I loved him! I had that same sense of pride that I'd had the day Julie was born. What had this child ever done to make me so proud of him? Absolutely nothing. I was so overwhelmed by love for him just because he was my child.

"Lord," I whispered. "May I always give them both this unconditional love. Teach me how, Father, to show them a love like only You can give."

Now our family was complete. This was what I had always dreamed of and prayed for. I had a husband who loved me and who I knew was a gift from God. God had blessed our marriage with two beautiful children who were healthy and wonderful. We were serving God in His ministry through the local church. I praised Him for His goodness! What more could any woman ever want or hope for? I had never been so happy. I had never been so full.

Weather Alert – Storm Ahead!

Chapter 5

It was a bright, beautiful, sunny Friday afternoon. Ryan was now five days old. Gary and I had brought our precious bundle of joy home from the hospital only three days before. Today was to be especially exciting because my mother was coming to stay for the weekend. My sister Ruthie, who lived with us at the time, was sunbathing from a pallet on our driveway, and she and I were discussing the idea of photographing our newborn.

I went into the house to phone Mama in order to ask her to bring her camera when she came to visit. I recognized the voice that picked up on the other end of the line when she said,

"First Baptist. This is Zillah."

My mom was the pastor's secretary at my home church and Zillah was a dear friend and co-worker.

"Zillah, this is Kathy Miller. Could I please speak with my mama?"

"Uh, Kathy, she isn't here right now." She continued on, "I don't know what's wrong, but your uncle Ronnie came by to see her, they talked for a few minutes and then she left to go home."

50

There was concern in her voice as she continued to emphasize that something was definitely wrong and that it had something to do with my daddy. I thanked her and quickly hung up the phone.

Immediately, I dialed the number to my parents' home. Mama answered. I began the conversation by explaining why I had made the first call (to get the camera), and then I questioned her regarding the information I had just received.

Mama began to inform me that she would be unable to come for the weekend and then, there was silence, as if she didn't know what to say next.

"What's wrong?" I asked.

"Well, your daddy's in some trouble."

Her voice had a sound of timidity as if she were trying to tell me someone had died. I continued to probe.

"What kind of trouble?"

Her only response was, "Financial."

She began to explain something about him owing a bank some money and needing to repay it by Monday. My "quick-fix" instinct started thinking of ways we could possibly help until she continued on telling me how much he needed. The amount seemed astronomical to someone with an average income.

"Oh, My!" We didn't have anything we could even sell that would come close to making a dent in that figure. What were we going to do?

I honestly don't remember if I began to cry at that moment, or if it was afterwards when I went outside to tell Ruthie what had just happened. I only remember the emptiness I felt inside and the hopelessness of being unable to help someone I loved so very much.

That night, Gary and I had been invited to go to dinner at the home of our dear friends, Chip and Sherry Dockins. Because of the circumstances, I really didn't feel like being around other people, but Gary thought it would be good for me, so I consented to go. Ruthie and her boyfriend, Rusty, had offered to baby sit our children; so, we went to dinner to try to enjoy ourselves, but throughout the entire evening, distress seemed to hang over me like a dark thunderstorm cloud.

When we returned home, I was so emotionally drained, I excused myself and went to bed early while Gary stayed up to talk with Ruthie and Rusty. It was then that they shared the news they had received just that evening as an update to the day's events. News, of which, I was still unaware.

Saturday mornings were routine for Gary as he would visit the children who would ride the church bus on Sundays. This Saturday was no different. While he was away, I tended to things at home such as making breakfast for Julie, Ruthie and myself. Not to be left out, Ryan began screaming, making it very clear that it was his turn to eat <u>again</u>!

I was nursing him at the time and as I sat in the rocking chair and caressed him to my breast, my thoughts were focused on Daddy. As I put myself mentally in his shoes, the thought came to me that what he was going through was the kind of drastic situation that just might drive someone to do something foolish. Instantly, I began to pray aloud,

"Oh God, please protect my daddy and don't let him do anything to harm himself." I cried as I prayed for somehow, in that moment, I sensed his pain.

Little did I know that my thoughts had been preparation for some very disturbing news I was about to receive. As Gary returned, he came into the bedroom and sat me down on the bed.

"I have something I need to tell you," he began.

The look on his face and the hesitation in his voice alerted me that something was very wrong and fear began to overtake me.

"I don't know how to tell you this," then he continued, "Yesterday, your dad tried to commit suicide."

"No, that's not true because my daddy has always said that anyone who would take their own life was obviously not in their right mind."

"Honey, it is true, but he's okay."

"But why would he do that?"

I reasoned that he must have been in a total state of desperation. This was all so shocking to hear!

"I have to go to him; you have to take me to be with him, please! I need to see for myself that he's all right."

We loaded the car and made the one-hour trip to my hometown. I didn't know what I would say when I saw him, but I knew I wanted to assure him of our love for him. I did have some questions, however. A part of me was angry with him for giving up and deliberately trying to leave us. I just couldn't believe he would do such a thing. My body seemed numb, but my mind was terribly alert and confused by the conflicting thoughts I was experiencing within.

When we walked into the living room, there sat my parents, as well as other family members and friends who had come to give their support. It was almost like someone had died. The air was chilling.

Our arrival did tend to ease the tension and lighten things up a bit. Everyone wanted to see and hold in their arms the new addition to the family. He was such a joy and the bright spot we needed to keep our lives going during this difficult hour.

The moment finally came when Daddy and I could share our thoughts with one another.

"Daddy, how could you have done this knowing that I had just given you a new grandson?" I began.

He responded, "I thought of that but rationalized in my mind the fact that since Ryan was so small, so young, he would have never known me; therefore, he would have never missed me."

"What about Julie?"

She had been the only grandchild for two-and-a-half years and the apple of her papaw's eye.

"She was the last person I prayed for before I asked the Lord to forgive me and closed my eyes to die.

I asked Him to give her a good, blessed life and to take care of her for me."

He couldn't say much more through choked tears. I wept to see him so beaten, so fragile.

"Then," he continued, "I lay there waiting to die. I began to feel peaceful, as if I was floating when I heard a voice. *The Voice* said to me, 'This is not the way out; it's not going to end like this.' At that moment, I became very sick and the sleeping pills began to come up."

He had swallowed seventy-two of them. By the time they found him, it was not even necessary to go to the hospital to have his stomach pumped.

After talking with him, it became apparent that Daddy's biggest fear was that of his family being embarrassed by the mistakes he had made in the past and the probability of them becoming public knowledge. He felt that getting out of our lives was the only honorable thing he could do at the time. You see, when the pressures of life seem insurmountable, we don't see the truth very clearly anymore. We see only from our perspective which is usually and often very clouded by the circumstances we are in.

If Daddy could have only seen the truth, what he would have seen would have been a family who loved him unconditionally. We loved him for who he was, our father (and husband, in Mama's case, of course). We weren't going to stop loving him because he had made a mistake. After all, true love and forgiveness go hand in hand. You can't have one without the other. God proved that to us when He sent Jesus. He didn't come for our goodness, but to forgive us for our sinfulness. He also didn't come to condemn us, but to save us sometimes even from ourselves. In like manner, for us to really love someone, we must do so in spite of all the faults and negatives they may have in their life.

I fear that, in today's world, we don't really know or understand much about this word *love*. We confuse many other feelings with it and label them with its name, but love is more than just a feeling with a fancy label. I suggest to you that love really does not exist unless it is unconditional.

I discovered something wonderful that spring day in 1982. Amidst any disappointment or heartache I might have incurred, I knew I loved my daddy...no matter what! I wanted him to know it then and I never want him to forget it. It isn't based on anything he has or has not done. It is because of who he is and that will never change.

This unforeseen nightmare that had seemingly just begun for Daddy and all of us would not be over for some time. There was an investigation which would take almost eighteen months to complete. During those months, Gary and I moved our family to South Carolina to begin a new ministry at a Baptist church in Greenville. It was there that we were interrogated by the FBI regarding Daddy's situation. It is a difficult position to be in when you know you must be honest, yet realizing that your honesty is helping to make a case against your own father. What else could I do? I had to do what was right.

I remember praying some of the most difficult prayers I have ever had to pray during this time. On my face before God, with tears, I begged God, "Oh God, please grant my daddy mercy and allow the court to pardon him with a suspended sentence."

After all, he had not stolen any money. But because of a desperate financial situation, he had borrowed it under false pretenses and therefore, illegal means. As much as I hated even thinking about it, I would pray, "But Lord, only you alone know what needs to be done to make him the finest man of God that he can be. I trust you, Lord. Do what is best for everyone involved."

Finally, in October, 1983, Daddy's court date arrived. We drove home to Tennessee to be with my family and support them during this difficult day. I remember calling Daddy into the bedroom early that morning.

"Daddy, no matter what happens today, I love you with all my heart and that could never nor will ever change."

He hugged me and we both cried. Then looking into my eyes, he acknowledged, "I'm ready for the judge's decision, whatever it may be. I'm just ready for the waiting to be over."

We drove to Knoxville and I sat quietly in the courtroom with the rest of my family and observed as Daddy pled guilty to his charges. The very elderly judge praised him for all of his reference letters from respected pillars of the community and state; for being a fine, respectable family man; and especially, for all of his years of selfless community service.

"But," he added, "I feel I must set a precedent. Therefore, I sentence you to one year and one day in a federal institution at which location shall be decided upon and conveyed to you at a later date." Those words cut through me like someone had stabbed me and drained the life from me; yet, I knew that God was in control and this was going to be the best thing for everyone's good, including Daddy because that is what I had asked for. My prayers had been answered, but it was a hard answer to accept. We would all have to learn to trust in Him.

It was November, just before Thanksgiving, when Daddy left for his reported destination in Montgomery, Alabama. It is a day I shall never forget. It was the blackest, bleakest day I had ever lived through. I guess that's really when my emotions began to plummet for it seemed that my world was crumbling before my very eyes. As a matter of fact, I can recall going to the doctor that day because I could not stop crying. When Dr. Miller (no relation, of course) walked into the room, he was instantly alerted from the mascara running down my stained, swollen face that something was terribly wrong.

"Tell me about it," were his first words to me.

"My dad left for prison today, and I'm not sure *how* to deal with it or if I *can* deal with it."

He continued further, "Do you think you're suicidal?"

"Truthfully, I don't know."

I was trying my best to be honest with both him and myself. "I just know I need something to help me 'snap out of this'."

He prescribed a mild nerve medication and a mood elevator and sent me home to hopefully deal with my pain. That was easier said than done.

How do you deal with the fact that your father, the man you've always had there for you, is in prison? Most people won't have to come to such a realization at any time during their lives and I certainly never thought that I would. Although I knew God had answered my prayers, even though in His sovereignty rather than in the way I perhaps would have chosen, I was angry for having to go through such an ordeal. In my gut, I just didn't have the energy nor did I want to face this "real life" situation.

As an added detriment, I became angry with myself because I was not handling my emotions in the way that I thought I should.

I told myself, "You are the wife of a minister. You're just supposed to accept this and go on with your head held high. YOU aren't supposed to fall apart. People are looking to see what kind of example you will be. That's not the way a true Christian living a life of faith would handle this situation."

Thankfully, there was a precious couple with whom we had become dear friends who took me under their wing and ministered to me in a special way during this time.

They advised me, "Kathy, you're putting too much pressure on yourself. Just because you are in the ministry doesn't mean that you can't allow yourself to be human. God understands your feelings and your broken heart. He is not disappointed in you for crying and being upset during this time of your life when you are experiencing such heartache."

My heart cried out with longing to believe their words were true, but my head kept repeating over and over again those lies of "Christian" self-sufficiency that I seemed to have somehow learned and adopted at some point in my past.

Not only did I hurt for Daddy and Mama and the rest of my family, but I was convinced that I was partly responsible for the grief they were experiencing. Over and over as they flashed through my mind, I remembered all the times I had cost them money due to my selfishness and need for attention...trips I thought I had to be a part of, college, extenuating medical costs (some really unnecessary), the dress for my senior prom, even the cost of my wedding. The list never seemed to end.

I hurt so deeply within and my mind somehow allowed myself to accept the blame. Suddenly, I knew I was the cause for their financial demise. I would carry this guilt with me silently for the next several years and it would gnaw at me like a never-ending predator on my soul.

Texas, Here We Come!

Chapter 6

We got through the holidays with great difficulty and then, only two months after Daddy's departure, we packed up our family and headed for the Lone Star state. Our destination would be Southwestern Seminary in Ft. Worth. Gary had been in full-time ministry for almost six years and had a desire to better understand the ministry to which he was called. He hoped that seminary would provide such answers.

It was so difficult leaving Mama now that she was alone, especially knowing the great distance that would be between us. We had never lived that far apart before and I couldn't bear to think of leaving her, even though I knew Ruthie would be close by and could be there for her. We knew this was God's plan for us at this time, however, so we stored our furniture and off we went pulling a U-Haul® behind us.

We took two days to complete the trip and when we arrived, I was ill prepared for what was awaiting me. A "two bedroom, furnished apartment" is what I checked on the application when we reserved our housing. There had been no pictures or I suppose no one would have ever gone.

"So, this is our new place?" I tried to sound as cheerful as possible. "Vinyl furniture. Well, I guess it'll be easy to clean while having two young children." We continued on with our initial tour of the place.

Through the living area to the left was the children's room which was conveniently stocked with bunk beds. If you could have looked with me, to the right, you would have seen another very basic bedroom. I surmised this to be the "master suite."

At first glance, the shock of what I was seeing was breath taking but after I had some time to adjust, I told myself and my family, "We'll fix it up and it'll be really cute. Just you wait and see." I don't think anyone was convinced, least of all, myself.

I've saved the best for last... the kitchen. That's a woman's haven, you know. Some haven! It was the tiniest thing you've ever seen. You could stand still and wash dishes, mix up your batter, and tend to the stove without ever moving from that one spot. That's the gospel truth. Oh, well, I guess there's something to be said for convenience. After all, we really needed to be looking on the bright side here.

"Gary, look at this. What's up with this oven?"

"I don't know. I've never seen anything like it. I think you have to light it or something. Yeah, that's it. You have to light the pilot light each time you go to use it."

"I don't think I like this. I'm afraid I'm going to blow the place up!"

"We'll learn how to do it and I'm sure it'll be fine."

Was he trying to reassure himself or me? I, for one, was holding my breath.

We made it a point to get settled as quickly as possible mostly for the sake of the children. We wanted them to feel secure in their "new home." Afterwards, we went out around the city trying to become a little more acclimated.

Our first weekend in the big city was a real adventure. First, our hub caps on our car were stolen while we were in a restaurant eating pizza. Secondly, I went to the grocery store and had an experience I will certainly never forget. When I looked up the aisle, there was a man "flashing" me. And to think, I was only looking for canned goods! Last, but not least, we were on our way to church on Sunday evening when we were pulled over by a policeman and ticketed for speeding through a college campus. We were so new to the area, we didn't even know we were near a college. We were beginning to wonder if God had really called us there after all, or had we got our wires completely crossed and misunderstood the directions?

- - - - - - - -

Each day, I would search the classifieds to see where I could begin in my search for a job.

"Here's one! An insurance agency."

The last job I'd had was at an insurance agency. Suddenly, I could see a glimmer of hope and a flicker of excitement surged through me.

"Honey, I just know this is going to be the one."

I made the call and set up the interview for that very afternoon. It was actually the first interview I had had at all. I went in all prayed up and as confident as one could feel after just being flashed a few days before. Lo, and behold, if he didn't hire me right on the spot! We were going to make it after all.

I reported for duty the very next morning. Everyone in the office was very kind in helping me "learn the ropes," and I began to fill my head with insurance information and new computer skills.

Then one day, a small unexpected incident occurred. My boss "accidentally?" bumped me with his hand in an area of my body that had been reserved for my husband only. Rather discrete was he in his effort to conceal what had really taken place. He apologized and although I felt quite uncomfortable about the situation, I told myself that it truly was an accident. Then, the accidents began to occur more frequently and it became apparent to me that these were really not accidents after all. By the way, he knew that my husband was a minister, but that didn't seem to matter to him. It certainly didn't deter him. I didn't know what to do.

This was long before the vocal days of sexual harassment and I found myself in a very difficult and uncomfortable situation. I did not tell Gary about it because I was afraid he would make me quit my job and I was the only one bringing in any money at the time. The bills had to be paid and my children had to be fed. That's all I seemed to be able to see at the moment. At least, that's how I rationalized it to myself.

I decided to commit the matter to prayer and that I did...a lot!

"Oh Lord, please help me. I don't know what to do. Will you please take control of this situation and help me out of this mess?"

A short time later, I came down with the flu. It was the sickest I had been in a long time, if ever. My temperature stayed at high levels for days and I missed a full week of work.

When I went back to work the following week, my boss called me into his office.

"Kathy, I need you to pack up your things and go home. I thought you were suited for this job but things just don't seem to be working out."

I was on the verge of tears, so I couldn't respond. I think I might have finally managed to say, "Yes, sir."

I remember it well because it was Valentine's Day. I was so devastated and humiliated! Nothing like that had ever happened to me. I had always been a good worker for any employer I had ever had and felt like I had especially given my all at this place of employment.

Then, I realized, "Dear God, you have taken control of this situation just as I asked you to do. I just didn't think you'd do it this way. What am I going to do now? I have to have a job." As if he didn't already know that!

I was excited to know that God had answered my prayer, but I really was questioning his methods at this particular time. The way it all turned out made me feel so embarrassed, and it totally destroyed my self-esteem. I became convinced I was not good at anything I attempted. Now, I had to go home and face my husband and tell him some very difficult things that I really did not want to say.

"Well, I lost my job today."

"What happened?"

"He just said it wasn't working out."

"Do you think it had anything to do with you missing work with the flu?"

"Yes, that and there's more."

After telling Gary the whole truth of what had happened and had been happening quite frequently at work, he was thankful that I had been removed from the situation, and was sorry that I had not told him about it sooner. I was very sorry about that, too.

We were going to have to trust God to take care of our needs and although it was very difficult at times, He did just that.

Gary had begun interviewing for positions at churches in the surrounding areas. Each time, I would go with him to the interview because we've always considered ourselves a team in the ministry. After all, God personally called me into the ministry just as he did Gary and when I married him, I knew that was where my ministry was to be...right by his side. He did have one interview while I was sick with the flu, however, and I was unable to be a part of that one. Wouldn't you know it? That's exactly the church where God called us to serve.

- - - - - - -

First Baptist Church, Midlothian, Texas. I had to practice memorizing it before I could even say the name of the town. After we had been at seminary for a short while, Gary came in one day and reported to me:

"Kathy, the church would like for us to move there and live, and then I would commute back and forth to the seminary for classes."

"Hallelujah!" "No more two bedroom, furnished apartment with vinyl coverings." I was thrilled!

We would actually be going back to Tennessee to get our own furniture and live in a real house like I had been accustomed to ever since we had first been married.

"Oh Lord, thank you for our new home to be."

We moved to Midlothian at the end of February and Gary began to serve on staff with the church on March 1, 1984. It was not a large church but it was full of musically talented and gifted people, so the possibilities for a wonderful music ministry were limitless. And what lovely people! We made some of the best friends we have ever had at any time in our ministry while we were there. What a blessing that would prove to be for it was during this time of our lives that my health began to decline.

Troubled Waters

Chapter 7

July, 1985, would be the time set aside for me to have a complete hysterectomy. I was really very excited about the surgery because I had experienced many problems for years due to endometriosis and ovarian cysts. This was going to be my answer for a new life free from the ills and pains to which I had become accustomed. The surgery went well and I recovered rather quickly. I was finally a new woman...or so I thought...

- - - - - - -

It was a pleasant Saturday evening in October. The party was to be such fun. Seldom did we get together as a staff for the sole purpose of having a good time, but tonight would be just that. We would all prepare our favorite dish, go to the pastor's home, eat to our heart's content and then top it all off with *Pink Panther* movies. We were in for a night of great fun and laughs.

As we were enjoying our meal together, sharp pain suddenly surged through my jaw as I attempted to chew my food. My hand went for my face making an unfruitful effort to quench the pain.

"Honey, I have that horrible pain in my jaw again. It's never seemed quite this bad before."

"Well, try to go ahead and eat. Maybe, it will go away."

I tried to continue my meal, but to no avail. I finally just gave it up and managed to endure the pain throughout the rest of the evening hoping not to spoil the fun. We said our good-byes and made our way home.

The next morning, I arose to begin my regular Sunday morning routine of getting ready for Sunday School and church. As I walked into the bathroom and looked into the mirror, I was horrified at what I saw staring back at me.

"Oh, my goodness!" I shockingly thought.

"My face is crooked!"

"Honey!" I screamed as I rushed into the bedroom, hoping Gary would tell me that I was imagining things.

"Honey, does my face always look like this?" It sounds like a silly question but I was very serious in asking. My chin was sitting to the left of my upper teeth and nothing matched up the way it should have.

"No, something is very wrong," was his reply.

The next day, our dentist took some x-rays and discovered that the bone on one side of my face near my jaw was much smaller than the bone on the other side.

"I want you to go see a friend of mine," Jerry said in his calm, soothing voice. "He specializes in TMJ," which we later found out stands for a disorder called Temporal Mandibular Joint Disorder. At that time, this was something we had never heard of but have learned through the years that many people seem to suffer from this disorder. We were about to learn a great deal about the matter.

We drove to south Dallas and when we arrived at the specialist's office, they took other types of x-rays, which determined that my jaw was definitely out of joint.

"We'll have to set it," he said. "It's going to be painful, so we'll give you an injection to put you into a 'twilight' state."

With reluctant voice, I somehow muttered "Okay."

Afterwards, they took impressions for the purpose of making a splint which I would wear at all times to ensure and maintain future alignment to the TMJ joint.

It was several days before the splint would be ready, and in the meantime, my jaw would not retain its proper position. Sometimes we would make several trips to the specialist in a day's time in order for him to realign my jaw over and over again.

Finally, the splint was ready. It was rather large and bulky with a long plastic extension which hung down from my upper teeth. It had to be long in order to catch my lower teeth and therefore, hold my jaw in it's proper position. As an added factor to being a constant nuisance, it also did not work as planned. My jaw kept finding a way to slip out of joint. Not only was I in constant pain, but now I was out five hundred dollars, as well.

The worst part of this whole ordeal for me was the fact that I was unable to sing. After all, wasn't that what I had been called to do with my life? Had I not gone to college for that very purpose? Now, I was in severe pain if I even dared open my mouth for any reason, much less the wear and tear that it would be on the joint to sing.

Our next step in looking for answers was to seek out an oral surgeon. We found ourselves in the doctor's office of Dr. Colin Bell who worked out of Baylor Hospital in Dallas. I will never forget our first visit with him.

"Hello, Kathy; Mr. Miller, I am Dr. Bell," he said with a smile as he shook both of our hands. "So, what's brought you here to see me today?"

As we explained the events of the past week or so, he had more questions:

"When did the problem first arise? Do you grit your teeth at night?"

There were many other questions of this nature that he needed answers to in order to make his assessment.

At last, the barrage of questions subsided. He then advised me to continue wearing the splint and since the problem had arisen so suddenly, he concluded that I would not be a candidate for surgery. On the other hand, he did order a series of other tests to confirm his prognosis.

The following week, I would have a tomogram , which is a special type of x-ray that shows the area under observation by sections. Also, an MRI was scheduled to reveal anything that might not have shown on the tomogram. All we could do was wait for his upcoming telephone call.

The call came one afternoon with unexpected results.

"Hello, Kathy, this is Dr. Bell."

"Yes, we've been waiting for your call."

"Well, we have the results from the MRI and frankly, I'm quite surprised because they are not what I had expected to find. I firmly believed from your examination and history that both of your discs would be in tact and that splint therapy would be sufficient, but the tests reveal that your right TMJ disc is completely worn through and totally damaged. We will have to get you in here for a consultation and schedule the surgery after all. For now, the left side appears to be okay and correcting the right side hopefully will allow the left side to remain unscathed."

Fearful, yet somewhat relieved that there was a prospective avenue of treatment, I replied,

"Thank you for calling. I will tell my husband."

The surgery was scheduled for January, 1986, right after the new year. I entered a luxurious suite at Baylor Hospital the evening before. I was given a steak dinner with all the trimmings, a kind of "last supper," if you will. Dr. Bell came in and explained everything he would be doing in surgery. He clarified the fact that he would make an incision in front of my ear, remove the disc and replace it with a piece of Proplast® which is made of a material similar to Teflon.® After answering any questions we might have had, he left for a good night's sleep and I was given a sleeping pill to ensure mine, as well.

- - - - - - -

"Good morning," the nurse sang as she turned on the light in my room. "How does it feel to be going home today?"

"Great" was my response while trying to smile through swollen cheeks and pursed lips.

"Go ahead and get your bath and you can go home, after you've seen the doctor."

"What time will he be coming by?"

"Oh, probably this morning sometime; but before lunch, for sure. You'd better get the move on before that handsome husband of yours gets here."

"Oh, all right." I couldn't wait to see him myself!

When Dr. Bell made his rounds, he gave us all the instructions we would need to follow when we got home and he gave us plenty of prescriptions to fill in order to enhance my recovery.

Lord, I'm Not Seeing This Clearly

Chapter 8

Since the surgery in January, I have recuperated wonderfully! It's hard to believe that I've completed all my physical therapy and I'm cruising through life every day aided by plenty of anti-inflammatory drugs, muscle relaxants and sleeping pills for bedtime. Dr. Bell says my range of motion is excellent and he's given me the "go ahead" for singing. I couldn't be happier. As a mater of fact, our Easter pageant is this coming weekend and we're doing a living cross.

It's the neatest thing. We had heard of living Christmas trees for choirs to sing on in December, so why not have a living cross at Easter to proclaim the message of Jesus' death, burial and resurrection? Gary designed it and some of our men from the church built it.

We're all so excited! Spring is almost here and new life is in the air everyday. The best part of the pageant, for me, is that I have a solo. I am able once again to praise the Lord with my singing, which I had at one time almost lost.

- - - - - - -

The Easter pageant has begun. Actually, all of the performances are now behind us except for tonight's presentation. I can't tell you how good it feels to sing again. Sometimes we forget how blessed we are until we have the absence of that very blessing. I guess it's our human nature to take things for granted at times, but how I wish we weren't that way.

"God, thank you for everything you've done for me. You are so good. Lord, I especially thank you for allowing me to praise you through song once again. These past few weeks have been like heaven on earth for me because I once again feel like I have purpose. I love you, Lord."

Tonight's presentation begins at 7:00 p.m. and everyone is in a frenzy behind the scenes. Cast members are busy with their costumes and make-up, while stage hands are making all the preparations that need to be made for this last evening.

As I'm standing on the living cross singing unto my Lord, I'm giving it all I have. We've reached the finale' and with as much power as my bright soprano voice will exude, I open wide to sing the final high "C."

"Oh, dear God, I just heard something pop in my jaw and although Gary has cut us off and the sound has stopped coming from my mouth, my mouth won't close."

The muscles were beginning to tighten up but somehow I was finally able to close my mouth. I was panic stricken as pain began to surge through the left side of my jaw. "This can't be happening," I thought to myself.

Those around me rushed to find Jerry, our family dentist who also sang in our choir. He went with Gary and me into a back room to see if he could figure out what had happened.

"I'm in a lot of pain" I tried to say through clenched teeth. Seems that once my mouth finally closed the muscles grew tighter and tighter and now it was as if my teeth were stuck together.

"Can you open for me?" was his next question.

"No." I shook my head, as I began to cry.

"I have some samples of an anti-inflammatory drug at my office. I can go get those for you to try and give you some relief, but we're going to have to call Dr. Bell's office and see about getting someone to see you."

Only Gary and I made the trip to Dallas for the emergency office visit that evening. When we got there, we were met, not by Dr. Bell, but by his associate, Dr. Allen. He had already informed us that Dr. Bell was on vacation in Hawaii.

"Hello Mr. and Mrs. Miller. I'm Dr. Allen."

"Have a seat right here." He pointed to the examining chair.

He took my chin into his hand and tried to open my mouth but got no results.

Then he said, "Let's try this." He picked up a tongue depressor and tried to insert it between my clenched teeth.

"I've never seen muscles this tight," he replied.

"We'll have to give you an injection of cortisone and see if that will give you any relief at all. I won't lie to you. It's going to be painful but I'll give you a little Novocain® first and maybe that will be helpful."

After the shot of Novocain,® I sat and squeezed Gary's hand as Dr. Allen inserted a long needle into the joint on the left side of my face. Tears streamed down my face and Gary, my sweet, precious husband cried along with me. All I could do was silently pray, "Oh Lord, please help me get through this." After completing the procedure, Dr. Allen said, "I'm so sorry."

It's not like it was his fault or anything but he was so compassionate and caring. You could tell he really felt concern for me. Believe it or not, it really was helpful to know that the physician caring for me was genuine in his manner of care in such a dark hour of my life.

"The next thing we need to do is wire your mouth shut until Dr. Bell gets back from Hawaii. That will be another ten days and then you will need to come to the hospital for another surgery, a disc replacement this time on the opposite side. I'll go ahead and schedule the surgery tomorrow and give you a call with the details."

That was just exactly what I did not want to hear; but hey, maybe this would finally get rid of these jaw problems for me. I'd do whatever needed to be done.

The next ten days were a real challenge. I could have nothing but liquids, of course, with my mouth wired shut. I became a real lover of soups and milkshakes during that time.

Dr. Allen's office called the next day to tell us that the surgery was scheduled for April 1. The previous surgery had been only three months before. I was ready to get it over with and go on with my life.

The first time I saw Dr. Bell was on the way to the operating room that morning. I remember it well because being April 1ˢᵗ, I told him not to be doing any "fooling" around while he was in there.

"What do you mean?" He looked at me kind of funny like.

"It's April Fool's Day," I said.

"Oh, Kathy, don't you worry about a thing," he said with his usual grin.

Then he added, "Do you have any questions before we begin?"

"Just one." "When will I be able to sing again?" He was careful in how he answered me.

"I'm not sure I can answer that right now. Let's just get this taken care of and go from there, okay?"

"Okay."

Then, it was "lights out" for me. The next thing I knew was that it was all over, at least as far as the surgery went. Now, I had to begin healing once again, continue with my daily routine of medications, as well as starting yet another round of physical therapy.

- - - - - - -

We've moved on a few months down the road and boy, am I ever glad of that! I'm still on several medications, especially for sleeping at night to ensure that I don't grind my teeth or tense up too much without being aware of it. I have a doctor's appointment this afternoon with Dr. Bell. You know, just a routine checkup. I can't wait to see what he says because he's always so encouraging. My progress has been remarkable as far as he is concerned. I'm opening my mouth wider than he ever dreamed I'd be able to. He's been very pleased, and so have I!

Gary and I sat in the waiting room until they called me in. Then, we went into the examining room and talked until Dr. Bell entered.

"Hello, Kathy, Gary." We were definitely on a first name basis by now.

"How are we doing?"

"Just great!"

"Have you been singing a lot?" he asked.

"Oh, yes, I'm trying to make up for lost time," I replied.

He looked at me with one of those smiles and said,

"You're always so positive, just like a ray of sunshine. You're an easy patient to treat."

"Well, thanks, that is so sweet of you to say."

It really made me feel good that I hadn't been a bad patient.

"Well, it's true. It's always a pleasure to see the two of you". Then he continued, "Let's see how far you can open today." He took out his small ruler that he always used to measure the opening.

"Good."

"Have you been in any pain?" he asked.

"No more than just occasional muscle spasms, as usual. I did want to ask you, though, about my sleeping medication. After I take it in the evenings, I can't remember anything that happens after that."

"What do you mean?" he wondered.

Gary then helped to clarify by saying, "Sometimes she'll clean the house and won't remember it the next day and she staggers all over the place trying to get undressed to put on her pajamas."

Then I added, "I'll wake up in the morning and think I went to sleep with my blue jeans on and wonder how I got dressed for bed."

"Those pills are too strong for you," he explained. "I wish you had told me sooner. You need to begin cutting them in half and let me know if it gets better."

"Okay."

He then continued on with the examination and commented further, "Before you go today, I'd like to take some more x-rays just to compare with your previous ones."

"All right."

I went with the nurse into the x-ray room where they did the panoramic x-rays and she started the machine. It went around my face and then, we were done. Quite painless.

After going back to the exam room, Dr. Bell returned after a short time.

"I'm concerned about some things that are occurring in regards to your bite. Have you noticed how your chin has receded somewhat?"

Gary and I looked at one another. We had noticed it but it seemed to be happening very gradually. I guess we had hoped it would just correct itself. I'm sure I was in a state of denial wanting so badly for everything to be all right.

Dr. Bell continued, "There's only one thing that I can think of that would be causing this to happen and that's why I wanted to do more x-rays today. I'm sorry to say that the x-rays have confirmed my suspicions. The ones at the temporal mandibular joints are deteriorating."

"What would cause that to happen?" was our question.

"The only explanation I have is that your body must be rejecting the implants that we have put in. I have been doing implant replacements for more than ten years, and this is the first time I have ever seen this happen."

Lucky me! People are always wanting to set records, but this one I wasn't too thrilled about.

"What do we do now?"

"We'll have to replace the deteriorated bones on both sides with something else."

"Like what?" I was beginning to be horrified.

"Well, we have two options. We can use two of your ribs, or we can put in prostheses, which are constructed of titanium steel. The good thing about using the steel is that your body will not reject them and you wouldn't have the ordeal of yet another surgery to remove your ribs."

I was speechless. I looked over at Gary as if to say, "I'm going to be sick." We left the office to go home and make the decision on which option to choose.

After a few days, Dr. Bell actually made the decision for us. He said that with the history of the bone deterioration, he didn't want to risk using bones from my own body or the same thing could happen all over again. It was going to be the titanium steel prostheses.

The prostheses had to be ordered and other arrangements made, so the surgery was not going to be until February, which was a couple of months away. In the meantime, I enjoyed singing in our choir's Christmas pageant, but during the entire time, I wondered if this would be my last.

Fast Changes

Chapter 9

During the months that we were waiting for my next surgery, a church contacted us to see if Gary would consider being their music minister. We went to visit them and after much prayer, we made the decision to go. They knew about my upcoming surgery and were willing to wait until after that for us to come on board.

Leaving a church is always very difficult, especially when you are loved as much as we were by the people at First Baptist, Midlothian. We had also grown to love them so very deeply. After all, they were the ones who had been there for us through all of my illnesses. We weren't near any of our family. They became our family, and a wonderful family they were! This move was going to be one of the hardest things we had ever done.

In the middle of February, I had nine hours of reconstructive surgery done. I thought I had experienced plenty of pain in my life, but the pain associated with this surgery topped them all. I would have rather had three hysterectomies than to go through this again. My head was literally the size of a basketball.

Gary brought Julie and Ryan to the hospital to see me. I don't remember much about it because I was so doped up, but I do remember that when they came, they stood backs up against the wall and were quite still. Gary told me later what they were saying, "Is that Mama?" They didn't even recognize me.

After coming home from the hospital, a going-away celebration was given in our honor, but I wasn't able to go. Some of our dearest friends came by our house to tell me good-bye. Saundra was the last one I remember.

"I brought you a little something," Saundra offered.

"Thank you. Oh, I love it!" I said as I opened the beautiful ironstone pitcher.

"Now, promise me you'll use it. It's not just for looking at," she said.

"Okay, I promise."

As we hugged each other good-bye, we both said, "I love you" and began to weep. The movers had packed everything up and we were to leave first thing the next morning.

March 1, 1987, only two weeks after my reconstruction surgery, our family of four began our two-day journey to Jacksonville, Florida. My head was still the size of a basketball, but I had plenty of medications to help me through the healing process.

- - - - - - -

We've been in Jacksonville for a few months now and Gary is on staff at the great North Jacksonville Baptist Church. The people have accepted us so graciously and made us feel very welcomed. Our pastor, Dr. Harold Hunter, is wonderful! We are growing so much in our faith and learning awesome things from the Word of God. It's like Dr. Hunter has a way of just making it come alive.

It has been slow recuperating from such a long, hard surgery, but physically, I have mended nicely. I've gone to a doctor here that Dr. Bell had recommended and he's very pleased with my progress. He sees no further need for me to have the sleeping pills or even the muscle relaxants, except occasionally. Everything has been fixed, I'm in good working order and life can get back to normal.

We've begun to get into a regular routine with the kids adjusting to their new school, choir practice on Tuesday evenings, Sunday and Wednesday church services, and making new friends with which to fellowship.

Today is Sunday and I am on the schedule to present the special music. I've chosen to sing an old song which I've sung for several years, but for some reason, it has really ministered to me this week while practicing it. It's called, "Whatever It Takes." Here are some of the words to the chorus:

"Whatever it takes to be more like you, Lord,

That's what I'll be willing to do...

I'll trade sunshine for rain,

Comfort for pain.

That's what I'll be willing to do.

So, whatever it takes for my will to break,

That's what I'll be willing to do."[1]

As I sang those words, I truly made it my prayer. I said in my heart, "Lord, I really mean this from the bottom of my heart. It's as though this is the first time I've ever sung this song. And, Lord, I really do want to be like you. I want to know you . Please show yourself to me."

That evening, during church, I got up to leave the choir because I felt like I couldn't get my breath. I must have blacked out for a short time because the next thing I knew, I was lying on the sofa in the pastor's office.

"Honey, honey, look at me." It was Gary's face I was staring at.

"Are you okay?" he asked.

I felt flushed and my heart was racing. I was trying to get oriented when I asked, "What happened?"

"You fainted. Here, drink some water."

My hands shook as I lifted the glass to my mouth.

"I don't feel very well. I'm shaky and I can't breathe."

In a few moments, the paramedics came in. Their station was right beside the church, so it didn't take long for them to get there. They took my blood pressure, checked my pulse and asked me a few questions. After some time, I was feeling better and they left telling me to rest a lot and follow up with my doctor.

The rest of the week I seemed fine. I was busy packing and getting ready to fly back to Texas to be in my best friend's wedding. Regina and I had become very close during the time that we lived in Midlothian and she had been single for those three years. We had prayed together many times asking God to send her the man that He had chosen for her to spend her life with.

She had just become engaged to Bruce right before we left. We both thought the timing stunk, but I promised I would come back for the wedding.

I was to fly out on Thursday morning, but first, while we were at church on Wednesday night, I started feeling all shaky and my heart began to race again. I went off in a corner by myself and begged God to help me.

"Lord, please help me. I don't know what's wrong and I can't stop what is happening to me. Lord, you know that if Gary knows about this, he won't let me get on that plane tomorrow and I've promised Regina. Please, Lord, do something! I really want to be there for her wedding."

I'm not really quite sure what happened after that, but I made it through that church service and went home to finish packing for my trip.

As I packed my things, I began to get really nervous about the trip. I had not flown very much and I had never flown by myself. I remember thinking, "If I just had some muscle relaxants or something to help calm my nerves, I think I would be okay."

I began to look through my collection of purses to see if I could find some old prescriptions; after all, I didn't take medications any longer. I was beginning to feel a little bit panicky when finally, I saw the bottle down in the bottom of the bag.

"Oh, thank goodness! Now, I can get on that plane."

The next morning, to make my reluctance even worse, we overslept. Gary was quick to begin awakening the entire family.

"Get up! Get up! We've overslept. The clock must not have gone off."

"Oh, no!" I was definitely in a panic now.

We managed to throw our clothes on quickly and drive to the airport just in time for me to catch the plane. I really didn't have much time to think about being nervous, but the first thing I did after checking in was to find a water fountain and take one of those precious pills I had found the night before. They were pain pills, but I figured that would help me relax enough to get through the flight. They did help and it was so nice to be able to enjoy myself, especially after all the tension I had had during the last week.

After we deplaned, Regina was waiting for me when I walked through the corridor to the airport. "Regina! I can't believe it's you!" I said as we embraced.

"I've missed you so much!"

"Me, too."

We went to retrieve my luggage and headed to the car for our trip to Midlothian. We ate lunch at a quaint, little home-style restaurant where we had such a wonderful time reminiscing and talking about her wedding day, her future, you know...all that girl stuff! Afterwards, she drove me to my friend Ronni's house where I would be staying during my visit.

It was also great reacquainting with Ronni and her husband Brian. We had fun laughing about old times and I was updating them on our new church and things that had happened since we had left. We had been gone now for four months.

The next day, there was so much to do getting ready for the rehearsal that was to be that evening. I was not only a bridesmaid in the wedding, I was also going to sing. For some reason, I was very nervous. It kind of made me mad because I had so looked forward to this and I wanted to be able to enjoy it.

The rehearsal went just fine and we all learned what we were supposed to do in the wedding ceremony the next day, and afterwards, I went with some of the "old gang" to one of our favorite restaurants in Ft. Worth.

While we were sitting at the table having a perfectly good time, suddenly that feeling came over me like I had previously had at church just earlier that week. I can only describe it as a feeling of panic. I didn't know what to do, so I ran to the ladies' room and tried to catch my breath. After a few deep breathing exercises, I went back to the table and took one of my pain pills.

Then, it happened again. The pill must not have been in my system long enough for it to have had time to work. It must have been more obvious by now that something was going on because Ronni accompanied me to the ladies' room this time.

"Are you all right?" she asked looking concerned.

"I don't know. Sometimes something comes over me and I just can't breathe. My heart begins to race and I feel as if I'm going to faint."

"Has this happened before?"

"Yes, but just in the last week or so. It only seems to feel like this when I get around a lot of people. It's just not like me. I don't even feel like me, anymore."

We talked for a few more minutes and I finally was able to go back to rejoin the group. She helped shield me from conversation until we could finally all leave to go home.

After getting back to the house, we all changed into our "comfies" and began to discuss what was going on with me. We delved a little bit into a past situation that had occurred during the time that we had lived there. For some reason, it seemed more upsetting to me than it did when it had actually happened. It was almost like it was happening all over again and I became very upset. My emotions absolutely got the better of me. The only thing I knew to do to help me get through this night was to take a few more of those pills, so I did.

Finally, they went to bed and I stayed on the sofa to watch TV and try to take my mind off of the subject. It just kept haunting me, so I thought a few more pills would help me forget. The next thing I knew, I found myself in chapter one of this book lying in the middle of Brian and Ronni's floor with paramedics and others all around me. "What on earth is happening to me?"

The next day was Regina's wedding and I wasn't about to spoil that for her, so I refused the urgency of the paramedics to go to the hospital. Plus, I've heard that getting your stomach pumped is not much fun. I was really scared.

Ronni had called Jerry and Saundra and they had come out in the middle of the night to be with us through the situation. No one understood what was going on including me, most of all.

Before the paramedics left, one of them told my friends, "Someone will have to stay with her every minute through the night."

They assured him that they would, but they had no idea what was in store for all of us. I was sick all night with the dry heaves and night sweats. No one got any sleep.

We all went to the wedding the next day just like nothing had happened. I look back now and I can't believe it. I did all of the things I was supposed to do, even sang a few songs, and I don't remember much about it at all. Regina never knew anything about the situation until she got back from her honeymoon a week later.

It was the day after the wedding that my friends began to realize something was terribly wrong. At least, it was then that they began to figure out what was wrong.

After the overdose, they had taken what was left of the pills out of my purse. Once again, I began to feel like I needed to be calmed down, but when I went to retrieve the pills from my purse, they were gone. I was so angry.

"Ronni, I can't find my pills."

"That's because we took them the other night," she said in a calm voice.

"Well, I need one now, so you can give them back to me."

"Kathy, there are no more pills."

"What do you mean?" I asked.

"We flushed them down the toilet," she explained.

"What did you do that for? Now, I don't have anything to help me when I need to settle down. What if I can't breathe again? I need those pills!"

I was screaming at her as I tore through her cabinets to see if I could find anything to take. She came over to me and took me by the hands and began to cry.

"Kathy, look at what you are doing."

"We think you have a problem and we want you to go talk to Greg."

"Greg?"

Greg was a Christian counselor that I had seen a few times after my hysterectomy when I suffered from a hormonal imbalance.

She continued, "We've already called him and he's agreed to see you today if you will be willing to go."

"On Sunday?" I was so shocked about the whole matter.

"Yes, he really wants to see you."

I don't know how they talked me into it, but I agreed to go and meet with Greg and my day was downhill the rest of the way.

After leaving Greg's office in Ft. Worth, he had convinced me that I needed to check myself into a mental facility for an evaluation in order to find out what was going on with me. I had never felt so despondent, so hopeless.

That evening, I called my pastor at our church in Jacksonville and told him what had happened and what I was about to do. I wanted him to know before Gary knew, so that Gary would have someone to turn to.

Dr. Hunter was so kind and assured me that everything would be fine, but I could not believe that in my heart. I was convinced that when Gary found out, my marriage would be over. I didn't think anybody could love me enough to go through something like this with me. He wasn't going to understand and I knew it. I didn't see how he could ever get over this thing I had done to him; this thing I had done to us.

I didn't even tell Gary. My friends called him to tell him and wouldn't let him talk to me because I was so upset.   I cried all night long and that is not an exaggeration.

I was in Midlothian, Texas.   My husband and children, then ages seven and five, were in Jacksonville, Florida. I wasn't sure how many miles apart that was, but I remembered that it took us two days to drive there. It must be a long way. I may as well have been on the moon because there certainly was a vast gulf between us in more ways than one.

On With Life

Chapter 10

I have been at the hospital now for several days. My psychiatrist's name is Dr. Cox. He looks like Albert Einstein and all of my friends here say that he looks exactly how they think a psychiatrist would look, whatever that means. Anyway, he's a nice man and I like him all right. He comes to see me every day and has started me on some medication called Deseryl.® He says it will take three or four weeks before I get the full effect of the drug, but it will begin to help me to some degree sooner than that.

My friends from Midlothian have once again become my family and someone comes to see me every day. They have been so wonderful. As a matter of fact, my 31st birthday is Sunday and if Dr. Cox will give me a pass to leave the hospital for awhile, they are going to have a pool party for me at Ronni's house. I only wish Gary could be here.

He and I have now talked about things. I am trying to explain to him why I was afraid to tell him about this mess I had found myself in; and he is trying to make sense of, if not all of it, maybe just one little piece of it. When he comes here to be with me, maybe we can work all of this out.

I have to be here for two weeks. Dr. Cox has advised Gary that I should be here the first week by myself and then it would be good for him to come out for the second week. Our sweet church is going to pay the cost for him to fly out here to be with me. God has been so faithful to us even though, for me, it has seemed that He is a million miles away. I'm trying to draw very close to Him, but at the same time, I feel so alone at times and wonder where He is.

In my last session with Dr. Cox, he asked me why I felt so alone.

"I just feel like no one loves me."

"Why do you feel that way?" was his next question.

"I don't really know why." That was all I could say.

"I want you to think about something for me. If no one loves you, why is your room so full of flowers?"

I really had to think about that. It was true. There were so many flowers in my room, it resembled a flower shop and I received stacks of cards from people every day. All of my fellow "patient friends" made comments every day about the amount of mail I always received.

I could entertain the thought that maybe I was loved after all, but I could not think of one reason why anyone should love me. If it was true, why did they? I had so much to sort out. Right now, I didn't even think God should love me, but I didn't know why I felt that way.

Gary called that afternoon with a surprise. "Hey, honey, how are you doing today?" He was so sweet.

"Okay, I think I'm getting better. I had a good session with Dr. Cox today."

"That's good. I'm looking forward to meeting him next week, and I sure can't wait to see you. I miss you so much."

"I miss you, too." Then, he continued.

"I have a surprise for you."

"You do?" It was the first time I had been excited about anything for some time.

"Yeah, it's your birthday present. I've sent it by overnight mail, so you'll be sure to have it for your birthday on Sunday. I can't tell you what it is, but it's small and you know that 'good things come in small packages.'" He almost sang the last part.

Oooh, I was so excited! I couldn't wait for the mail to come tomorrow!

Jewelry has always been a way to my heart; I've loved it since I was a little girl. Surely, that's what had to be in a small package. It was hard for me to close my eyes that night because I could hardly wait for tomorrow to arrive.

"Good morning," the nurse said as she brought my breakfast to me.

"Did you sleep well?" They would always ask.

"Yeah, I think maybe I did for once," I said to my surprise.

Then, I asked her as I opened my juice, "What time does the mail get here today?"

"Oh, the mail doesn't run on Saturdays," she said rather nonchalantly.

"What?! But I have a package that is supposed to be here today. My husband sent it overnight just so that I would get it today." I thought my heart was going to break. My whole day was ruined.

"Well, I think that they might deliver it to the hospital on Saturdays, but it stays in the mailroom until Monday," she was explaining further.

"Can you please find someone to let me into the mailroom, so that I can have it, if it's there?" I was pleading with her.

"I'll see what I can do."

She did work it out for an orderly to take me to the mailroom and my small package was there, after all. It was the most beautiful marquise cut amethyst ring surrounded by diamonds. That isn't my birthstone, of course, since I was born in July; but we had looked at rings a while back, and I really liked an amethyst that we saw. This was even better because it was one that he had picked out himself. I was the envy of the whole ward! I was just so happy to have something from my precious husband that showed that he still loved me in spite of all the things that had so recently transpired.

- - - - - - -

I did get my pass to leave the hospital on Sunday and all of my friends came to Ronni's for my party, all except for Susan. She was with her family on vacation in Washington. We had so much fun! I am actually starting to "lighten up" a little when it comes to talking about what I've come through over the past week.

It's hard to believe that I have been here in the hospital exactly a week today. It's Monday morning and my precious husband, my partner is coming today. I'm so excited, but a little nervous at the same time. I've told everybody here about how handsome he is and how wonderful he is, and they all want to meet him. It's odd how close I have gotten to some of the people here. I guess we're all in the same boat, so to speak, so that gives us a bond that's hard to put into words.

It's been pretty strange the way God has been able to use me to minister to the people here. I asked Ronni to bring me a tape recorder and some accompaniment tapes and I began to sing for everybody. We have a large room where we all congregate to talk, watch TV, play games and such. I sing for them there. Their most requested song is "Whatever it Takes." Isn't that amazing? That's the same song I had sung at church just before I left to come out here. That was only eight days ago. It seems like a lifetime.

The other night, one of the ladies asked me if I would speak to her daughter and tell her about the Lord. I think she has had a lot of problems which have affected her and maybe influenced her into making some bad decisions in her life. They came into my room one evening and we began to talk.

"Hi, Kathy, this is 'Mary', Linda said to me.

"Hi, Mary. It's so nice to meet you. I've really enjoyed getting to know your mom some."

She seemed quiet but managed to answer, "Yeah, she's told me about you, too."

We talked some more and I began to share with her about my faith in Jesus Christ. I explained to her that even though I was going through a really difficult time in my life that I knew Jesus was there with me and that he would never leave me. I was saying the words with my mouth, but I think I was trying to convince myself, too, of that very truth down in my heart.

"Mary, do you think you would like to accept Jesus Christ into your heart and have a personal relationship with him?"

She very politely replied, "No. I don't think I'm ready for that."

I wasn't expecting what happened next. Linda looked up at me with tears in her eyes and said, "I do."

I couldn't believe it! God had turned this thing around and the one I thought knew the Lord was the one asking to know Him.

So, if I needed to look for some kind of silver lining in all of this, I think someone coming to Christ would definitely be at the top of my list. Even though I don't understand it all, I trust God that He is in control and I thank Him for using my messed up life for His glory. Who, but God, could do such a thing?

Gary came in on the afternoon plane. One of our dear friends from Midlothian picked him up at the airport and gave him a car to use to go back and forth for the week. He is even staying at their home so that we will not be out the expense of a hotel. What a blessing these people are to our lives! I remember seeing him as he walked through the door.

"Oh, I can't believe it's you!" I said as I threw my arms around him. Everyone was watching. It was like the moment we'd all been waiting for.

"You look great," he said to me in a surprised voice.

"Thanks. I tried to get all prettied up for my man. Thank you so much for my ring, it's absolutely beautiful. I've shown it to everybody whether they wanted to see it or not."

He laughed as he said, "I 'm sure you have."

I introduced him to everyone and then, we went to my room to spend some time together and to talk. I remember our first conversation once we were together.

"Kathy, I've been thinking all the way out here about how I would say this, but I think we've been fooling ourselves."

I was scared after that statement.

"What do you mean by that?" I asked, even though I wasn't sure I really wanted to know.

"We've always said that we were best friends, but if that was really true, I would have been the first person you called when you were in trouble. I don't think you think of me as your best friend."

"But that's not true...I"... He interrupted me to go on. "Let me finish."

"Okay."

"I think it's really my fault. Before we got married, your daddy had protected you your entire life because he loved you. Well, I love you, too, so after we got married, I took over where he left off and I began trying to protect you, just like he did."

"What's wrong with that?" I asked him.

"I think that you think of me like I'm your daddy. Instead of wanting to call me when you were in trouble, you were afraid to call me. It's like you were afraid I was going to give you a spanking or something like a parent would do."

Boy, did he strike a nerve! I really did not want to admit it, but he had hit the nail on the head. I really did see him in that way, but I never knew it until now. We decided from that point on, things were going to be different. We were going to work on our relationship and truly become best friends. He became very careful about shielding me from hurtful things but began to always share with me the whole truth about situations, no matter how hard it might have been; and I began to learn how to deal with life's problems in a new way, without the misuse of pills.

After spending the week together working on issues in sessions with Dr. Cox, he released me to go back to Jacksonville, but first he gave Gary a few instructions:

"Don't make any life-changing decisions while she is in this condition."

"Remember that she has acute clinical depression. She feels like she's in a hole. All she can see right now is the darkness of that hole surrounding her. After a while, the medicine will work and she will be able to climb out."

"Remember that perspective is truth to her right now. Even though she is loved a great deal, as long as she believes she isn't loved; then for her, she isn't loved. Be patient. She is improving but it could take a great deal of time. Help her to work through this."

With all of this advice taken into account, we went to board our plane. I was going home to be with my family once again.

Adjustments

Chapter 11

"Mama!" I heard as I walked through the front door of our townhouse.

"Oh, I missed you so much!" I squeezed them so hard, I never wanted to let go. I was home. Oh, it was so good to see my babies.

We began to try to get back into a routine and make everything as normal as possible after our lives had been so disrupted. It was really hard for me. It seemed as though I'd been in a bad nightmare or that I'd been away performing in a play or something, and I didn't really know how to act now that I was thrust back into what was supposed to be normal. I wasn't sure what my role was any more as a wife, a parent, or even a person. I felt as if I was supposed to resume life as usual, but I was different somehow.

So much had happened, and I was also afraid of how people at church were going to react towards me. They had been told I was in the hospital, but I'm not sure they really knew for what reason.

I continued taking the anti-depressant daily, but now I had to find a psychiatrist in Jacksonville to take over my care. That was not a very easy thing to do. The doctor we found wasn't familiar with the anti-depressant that Dr. Cox prescribed for me, so he changed my medication right away. Now, I had to start all over again waiting for the medication to get into my system. Antidepressants take four to six weeks. So, here we go again.

When I went back for a follow-up two weeks later, we discussed my medication in detail.

"I don't want to take this medication. You're going to have to give me something different," I began the conversation. "Be patient" was his response. "You haven't given it enough time."

"I have gained fifteen pounds in the last two weeks. If you think I was depressed when I came in here before, I'm really depressed now. Can't you put me back on the Desyrel?"® I was doing fine on it and I was fifteen pounds lighter." I was pleading my case.

"I just don't feel comfortable treating you with something I'm not that familiar with, but I will give you something different." And so, my medication was changed, yet once again. We were back to square one.

Going back to church was hard. I always felt like people were staring at me. I don't think they really were, but that was my perception, so it was real for me. I got to where I didn't want to go if I could get out of it. I didn't like to drive or get out much any more than I had to.

I became frustrated with my new doctor and began to look for another one. Someone recommended a Christian psychiatrist, so I called and scheduled an appointment.

He was a nice man, but I did not progress very well with his method of treatment. I had learned to talk about things with Dr. Cox, in Texas, and found it very helpful. This doctor never let me talk. He would just say, "Take your medicine, and you will get well." And he would always add, "Just thank God for his grace."

Well, I do thank God for his grace, but he seemed to trivialize it somehow and going into his office week after week, only to hear, "Take your medicine and you'll get better" wasn't doing a thing for me.

As much as I was trying to live a "normal" life, whatever that is, I began to feel very despondent again. I became full of fear and dreaded nightfall. When the sun would go down, so would my spirits. I was weepy all the time and I hated feeling this way. I felt like I had no one to help me.

Finally, our pastor called and got me into the Mayo Clinic of Jacksonville for a complete psychiatric work-up. Dr. Merrit was the overseeing psychiatrist for that department. He was just wonderful. I really liked him, and I felt like he genuinely wanted to help me. He, too, was a Christian man which meant a great deal to me.

Now, when I say a complete work-up, I mean complete! There were the infamous ink blots.

"What does this look like?" Yeah, they really do use those things.

Then, there was the IQ test. I have no idea where I rated on this one, and I don't think I want to know. I don't need someone to tell me that I'm not brilliant. I figured that out a long time ago.

There were questionnaires that went on for days, even medical tests that examined the functions of my brain. After the evaluation was completed, they brought us in for an explanation of the results.

"Mr. and Mrs. Miller, after a complete and thorough evaluation, our conclusion is not definitive," he explained.

"What do you mean?" We were a little confused.

"Well, according to Kathy's test results, there is the possibility that she has either a personality disorder or bipolar disorder."

He went on to explain in further detail exactly what each of those was. I'm not really sure I grasped the meaning of the personality disorder, but I understood what bipolar disorder was when he described it as being recognized by extreme mood swings. I had previously heard it referred to as Manic Depressive Disorder. That sounded very scary to me, but he felt like either scenario could be controlled with proper medication. Actually, the medication he was prescribing for me to take would take care of both illnesses.

I went home to begin yet another proposed method of treatment. Let's see, how many does this make now? I believe the answer to that is four and that is within a time span of only two months. Needless to say, things got worse before they got better. The fears were excessive, I never wanted to get up in the morning because I dreaded feeling fearful and depressed all through the day. I knew I was being a horrible wife and mother, and I hated my life the way it was. Finally, I telephoned Dr. Merrit and in a few hours, he returned my call.

"Kathy, this is Dr. Merrit."

"Thank you for calling me back." I was crying.

"What's going on?" he asked.

"I'm just not thinking right. I don't want to live like this anymore."

"Now, I need you to be honest with me, Kathy. Have you had thoughts of taking your life?"

"Yes, but I don't really want to die. I just don't want to feel like this anymore. When is it going to get better, or is it? Is there any hope for me because right now, I can't see any." By this time, I was sobbing.

"Here's what I think we need to do. We need to get you into a hospital just until we can evaluate you long enough to get your medicine under control. Are you willing to do that?" he asked.

"I don't know, I guess. I really can't think right now. I'll talk to Gary and have him give you a call." Then, I hung up the phone.

"Oh, God, I can't believe this," I prayed. "Here we go again. Is there any hope for me? Please show us what to do."

After Gary talked with Dr. Merrit, he gave us a choice of going to the mental health ward of a local hospital, or to go to a treatment center specializing in mental health at St. Simons Island, Georgia. It was only a short drive away. We decided on St. Simons, so that I would be away from people at the church. We were afraid that if I was at a local hospital, people would want to come and visit me, and I just did not want people to see me this way. Dr. Merrit made the arrangements and told them that I was coming.

Gary drove me up there that very day. It was a pretty quiet ride. I didn't know what to say. I do remember thinking, "I'm going to make the best of this. I have to do this for me and I have to do this for my family."

He reassured me that he was on my side and supported me one hundred percent. It sure was good to have him by my side this time.

They took us into a room where I was informed of my rights and made aware of their policies.

"You understand that you are signing yourself into this facility?"

"Yes." I did understand.

"And you understand that once having signed these forms, you have agreed to the full course of treatment and once your husband leaves, you cannot change your mind and sign yourself out?"

It sounded harsh, but I said, "Yes."

"You will be required to attend group therapy and classes each day and you may not use the telephone except at designated times. Do you understand?"

"I do."

"Your family can only come to visit after you've been here a certain amount of time and then, only on designated days and times."

"Okay."

"You may not leave the premises at any time without proper supervision."

I was wondering how many more guidelines there were.

"Finally, you must keep all belongings believed to be harmful to yourself in a basket assigned to you and when needed, you may check them out under supervision."

I did not want to sign on the dotted line, but I knew I had to if I was ever going to get better. Then, they took me and assigned me my basket. They kept my curling iron, razors, belts, even all of my makeup. I was told I could have my makeup each morning as long as I was not alone when I put it on. That was because of the mirrors.

They were afraid I would cut myself with them. I promise you, they think of everything!

"Now, it is time for your husband to leave. You may say goodbye and then you will have to come with us."

It sounded so much like I was being taken to prison, and I guess that at this time in my life, I was a prison to myself.

Gary kissed me and told me he loved me and then, I stood and watched him walk out of those double doors we had just walked through. They locked shut and there I stood, alone. It would be days before I would see him or the children again.

Complete But Not Whole

Chapter 12

They had told me when I entered the hospital that the prescribed course of treatment was three weeks, but my doctor went on vacation and I ended up having to stay for four. What is it with me and doctors always being on vacation, anyway? But, finally, I had finished my tenure and was ready to go home.

I learned some really good things during my stay there like how to take care of myself and how to deal with conflict. Really helpful stuff. But the main thing that they helped me with was how to be honest with myself about my feelings. We really do lie to ourselves at times, don't we? And we learn to believe our own lie. I discovered while I was there that I had been angry with God about many things that had happened to me in my life. I think I knew it all along, but I was so afraid to be honest about being angry with a holy God. I was brought up to believe that you could not do that or there would be dire consequences. After releasing some of that anger, I was able to free myself of the hurt it had been causing me for such a long time. I was even able to remember Bunchie again, which brought so much joy to my life and I had been missing out on that joy for fourteen years.

They also helped me admit to my dependency on prescription drugs. I did not think I was addicted because I did not have a strong physical addiction, but what I discovered was that addiction is really in the mind. As long as I wanted them and depended on them to make me feel better, even emotionally, I was addicted.

I was now going home a much healthier individual both mentally and emotionally. It really had been an effective course of treatment in many ways and I was looking forward to the quality of my life improving greatly.

I still had a long way to go, but I was going to take it slow and seek God every day to help me along the way. The one thing that still had not been overcome was my fears.

- - - - -

"Home, sweet home," I thought as I began a new day. I took my Bible out and began to speak aloud to the One who wrote it. "Lord, I have always been taught that every answer to every problem in life can be found in the pages of this book. I've always believed that, Lord. Now, I want to ask you to prove that to me. God, if what is wrong with me can be explained somewhere in here, I am asking you to show it to me, and I'll not stop looking until I have found it."

The thought occurred to me that the apostle Paul had a "thorn in the flesh," as he so eloquently describes in his writings. That's where I decided to begin my search.

"Okay, here it is. 2 Corinthians 12:7... 'there was given to me a thorn in my flesh, a messenger of Satan to torment me.'"*NIV®*

"Could it be, Paul, that your thorn could have been depression? After all, it does torment the soul," I thought.

"I know that you pleaded with the Lord three times to be delivered from this torment, but you got another answer... 'My grace is sufficient for you, for my power is made perfect in weakness.'" 2 Corinthians 12:9*NIV®*

I began to delve a little deeper into a few more passages of Scripture when a verse just seemed to jump off the page. It was 2 Timothy 1:7 which reads:

"For God did not give us a spirit of fear, but of power and love and a sound mind."*NKJV®*

"Wait a minute Lord, Your word tells me that You did not give me fear, but I have fear. I'm consumed by it."

He whispered back to me, "I didn't give it to you."

I continued to search the Scriptures. I sought long and hard. It was like I was on an Easter egg hunt looking for the prize egg. There are a lot of wonderful things to be found in the Word of God, but I kept on coming back to this same verse over and over again. So, I looked even closer.

"Okay, God, it says here not only that You didn't give me fear, but that You did give me some other things like power, for instance. Well, then where's mine? I don't have power. I have never been so weak."

I was really going to have to chew on this for a while.

"Now, the next thing this verse says is that you came to give me love."

It was then that I began to weep. There were all of those feelings that I did not understand. Why did I not feel loved? I poured my heart out to Him.

"Lord, I don't feel loved by anybody, not by Gary, nor the children, not even by You. I know I've trusted You as my Lord and You sent Your only son to die for me to prove Your love for me, and I don't have the right to ask for anything more, but Lord, I am asking. I don't know what else to do. You are the only One that can help me and I need to be able to feel your love for me."

There was no answer this time, but I felt better, almost as if I had been cleansed. I realize now that I had been "washed by the water of his Word."

Ephesians 5:26$_{NIV}$®

As I looked further into that verse from 2 Timothy, there was a third thing that God says he gives to us...a sound mind. I nearly had to burst out laughing at this point when I caught myself saying out loud, "What a joke!"

"Lord, if you've given me a sound mind, then there must be a new definition for the word *insane*."

By the time I had made my way through this verse, I had pretty much dissected it thoroughly. I gave myself a quick review and came up with this summarization.:

"Okay, Lord, if I am seeing this clearly, then what You say You give to me, I don't have. On the other hand, what You say You don't give to me, I am so controlled by, at times, that I can hardly function. Sounds to me like my whole life is backwards, turned upside down."

That was a pretty good description of how my life had been the last few months. I still didn't understand fully what He was saying to me, but I knew He was trying to show me something. Something I desperately needed to see. I was slowly beginning to see a tiny bit more clearly piece by piece. Maybe I had made a small breakthrough. At least, now, He did not seem quite so far away.

Healing

Chapter 13

I must have read 2 Timothy 1:7 at least a thousand times, or so it seemed. Every time I'd try to study my Bible for any reason, I would always end up back there. I was just waiting for the light bulb to come on and illuminate whatever it was I was missing.

Our church began a series of evening meetings during my search for what was missing. A man by the name of Rocky Freeman was preaching. He is a Jew who has converted to become a believer in Christ. He is so full of Biblical knowledge and understanding that it is truly amazing. We didn't really advertise these meetings and the choir isn't singing, but each night when Brother Rocky gets up to speak, the church is fully packed. It's really been a rather remarkable sight.

He has been speaking on subjects I have never been exposed to very often, such as spiritual warfare. Oh, I've always been taught that Satan is real, but no one ever really made me aware of the fact that I needed to stand my ground against him. For some reason, that is something that just never made it's way into any of my doctrinal teaching.

I had gone to every meeting thus far, but I just didn't feel up to going tonight. It's Wednesday, the last service, but I've had one of my "bad days." Sometimes, I still have trouble being around other people. I've become very introspective as I've tried to figure out what is wrong with me, and I just want to spend time with the Lord, alone. I feel like He is the only one who could ever begin to understand my inner pain.

When Gary came home after church, he sat me down and said he needed to talk with me about something.

"Honey," he said. "Brother Rocky came to our staff meeting at church earlier today and he talked with us about how the devil has a plan to destroy God's children, especially those of us in His ministry. I've always known that, the Bible teaches it, but as he was speaking today, it hit me, 'I think that is what is happening to Kathy.'"

He went on to say that Brother Rocky had spoken to them about husbands taking spiritual authority over their homes. He taught them how to pray for their families' protection and gave them some very useful tools on how to teach them to be aware of the Enemy and his ploys.

"Honey," he said to me. "I think the enemy is doing his best to destroy you, our marriage and our ministry."

As Gary spoke, I began to sob uncontrollably. I knew that this was the time and the place for which God had been preparing me. I tried to speak through the tears.

"I know. God has been trying to show me that for weeks."

I had not yet shared with Gary about the verse in 2 Timothy because I didn't want his input on what God might be trying to tell me through it. Not that I don't value his insight, he has great wisdom, but I wanted God and God alone to show me what He was saying to me.

I got my Bible which was already open to the verse.

"Look, look at what this says. The Lord has been telling me that fear is not what he wants for me and everything that he does want for me, I don't seem to have in my life right now."

I was crying so hard that I was shaking. Gary took me in his arms and held me as I tried to make sense of this moment in time. Then, he looked me closely in the eyes and asked, "Will you let me pray for you?"

Oh, how I wanted him to pray for me, but I can't describe to you the great fear that came over me at that very moment. I was trembling. It was as though all the forces of evil poured out on me as much fear as I had ever known. All I could do was nod my head, "Yes."

We went into our bedroom and knelt beside the bed. He put his loving arms around me and began to pray with authority as the priest of our home.

"Oh, God, we are coming to you, Father, as your children. Lord, I love Kathy, and I know that you love her, too. Lord, she has been through a horrible ordeal lately and it hurts me to see her this way."

I was on my knees with my head buried in his shoulder sobbing. All I could think of was how much I wanted to know and feel the love of God in my life.

"Please, Lord, show Yourself to me and touch me with Your love."

Gary continued praying, "Lord, if what has been happening to her is from You, then Lord, we will accept it but please, give us the grace to endure it. But Lord, if what is happening to her is an attack from the Enemy, then we stand against it in the name of the Lord, Jesus

Christ and we ask You to remove it from her right now! Now God, we trust You and will accept whatever You have for our lives, as long as we know it is from You."

I am not exactly sure how I can tell you what happened to me that night beside our bed. In an instant, I felt so clean, so pure. I knew I was in the presence of a holy God, and I **knew** that **He loved me**! I felt so light, so free; I just wanted to fly. I had been touched anew by the hand of God.

It was the first night in a long time that I was not afraid to go to bed and close my eyes for the evening. It felt so good to finally rest peacefully.

The next morning was awesome! I actually wanted to get up and I looked forward to the day that lay before me, unclaimed. I wanted to live because I had no more dread of the future. I couldn't wait to go to our church to tell our pastor and others what had happened to me, but I did not have to say a word. They knew something was different when they looked into my eyes.

There have been many times since that night I was delivered from fear, that I've questioned God about how he made me. I'm such a "feeling" person. As a matter of fact, several years ago, Gary and I took a personality profile where the results rate you as a "feeling" versus a "thinking" type of individual. I did not answer one question on the entire test in the "thinking" category. It was reported to us that they didn't even have a score for me because I was off the scale. They said that only three percent of the entire world would answer the questions in the same way that I had answered them. Feelings are just a major part of my life. They are a very vital part of who I am. And sometimes, I have hated that. It is a hard thing to be so sensitive, but God has been so patient with me when I have become dissatisfied with who I am.

I'm thankful for a God who is willing to meet us right where we are, no matter where that may be. That's what he did for me, and he'll meet you right where you are, too.

I love the account of Thomas in the Bible when the disciples come to him after the resurrection of Christ and tell him that Christ has risen.

"He's alive! We've seen him for ourselves," they proclaimed.

Thomas replied, "Unless I see the nail marks (prints) in his hands and put my finger where the nails were, and put my hand into his side, I will not believe."

John 20:25*NIV®(Parenthesis mine)*

We are so quick to criticize poor Thomas. We've even given him the title "doubting Thomas." But Jesus did not condemn him for his unbelief and lack of faith. Instead, He came and met Thomas right where he was. Jesus appeared to him a week later and said, "Thomas, put your finger here; see my hands. Reach out your hand and put it into my side." At that very moment, Thomas' eyes were opened and he saw the Lord.

His reply, "My Lord and my God!"

John 20:27,28*NIV*®

That's how I felt the night he met me in our bedroom. I truly saw him just as Thomas did and I could only say as he did, "My Lord and my God!" He was finally more real to me than I ever could have imagined He could be. He met me at the point of my need. He knew I needed to feel his love. After all, He made me like I am, feelings and all. One thing is for sure, I feel His love now, and I will never be the same.

New Life, New Joy for a New Day

Chapter 14

It's been over twenty years since that eventful January evening in 1988. I only mention the date because in the Bible, numbers have great significance. For instance, when God was about to do something really great, there would always be a preparation time of forty days. The number *3* in the Bible represents the Trinity: Father, Son and Holy Spirit. Six is the number used to refer to man; God made man on the sixth day. Seven is the number of complete perfection; God created the world in seven days. And the number eight is representative of new beginnings. The first month in the year 1988 was the beginning of a new life for me.

I know the Lord in a much deeper way than I ever did before. He is so real to me. I think about the life of Job and all of the heartache he went through but in the end, Job proclaims,

"My ears had heard of you but now, my eyes have seen you." Job 42:5*NIV*®

I think back to that Sunday in July of 1987, when I sang "Whatever It Takes" and remember my prayer,

"Lord, I really want to know you, so whatever it takes to be more like you, that's what I'll be willing to do."

He knows the desires of our heart and He knew I meant what I sang that day. He was faithful to grant me that desire and the true story you have just read is what it did take for me to know Him...truly, truly know Him.

I never want to go through it again, but I can honestly say that I would because of the riches I have received from knowing Him in a more intimate way. For so long, his love for me was like a deeply buried treasure. Now, however, I long to scatter this precious treasure on top of the sand shining in the light of the Son for all the world to see.

My life has changed so greatly that I can hardly remember the person who has walked through the pages of this book. Yet, I never want to completely forget her because she reminds me of the grace and goodness of God in my life.

Just as, "the Lord blessed the latter part of Job's life more than the first," Job 42:12$_{NIV}$® He has done the same for me. Being able to be free from fear and bondage of my past, which once plagued me, I now live a life of hope. "For I know the plans I have for you," declares the Lord, "plans to prosper you and not to harm you, plans to give you hope and a future."

Jeremiah 29:11_{NIV}®

Has it always been easy?

"Heavens, no!"

Have I ever wanted to give up?

"Many times."

Do I still struggle with depression?

"I take medication every day because of a chemical imbalance in my brain." The Lord has shown me that that is no different than a diabetic taking insulin to supplement what her body does not produce.

Even though I will always wrestle with this illness called depression, and there will always be hills to climb and valleys to go through, the one constant that I have in my life, which I received from Him on that appointed night in 1988 is this: I know that He loves me...so much that He would meet me in my room and make Himself known to me at the time I needed Him most. Call me a "doubting Thomas" if you wish, but now I have seen the Lord.

Now, I live a life free from fear with peace in my heart. The Bible says, "For He Himself is our peace.

Ephesians 2:14_{NIV}®

He showed Himself to me in a wonderful, real, marvelous way and His peace came with Him. There is nothing like the "peace of God which (goes far beyond) all understanding."

Philippians 4:7 NIV®(Parenthesis mine)

Since that day, I look forward to the setting sun which I so used to dread. Actually, it is now my favorite time of day.

I have learned to be honest with God about my feelings and to share them with Him, even if that means being angry with Him. He's a big God and He can take it. Besides, if I'm not honest with Him, I am only fooling and hurting myself because He already knows how I feel, anyway. The book of Psalms, chapter 139, which has become one my favorite passages of Scripture, says in verse 4, "Before a word is on my tongue, you know it completely, O Lord." NIV® He is such an awesome God. Who do we think we're kidding when we try to keep anything from Him?

God desires a relationship of openness and honesty with me just as I desire a relationship of openness and honesty with my husband; which, by the way, has improved our relationship tremendously since those earlier years. Now, he truly **is** my best friend. He is the first one I call if I am in trouble.

My friend, I don't have all of the answers, but I have learned a great deal through my experience of life. One thing that I do know is that God desires a real, alive, thriving relationship with you and me.

I'm always hearing people say, "I need a new lease on life." If that is you, I want you to know that you can have it. Jesus said, "I have come that you may have life and live it to the fullest."   John 10:10$_{NIV}$®

The reason He came to this earth, lived a sinless life, died for the forgiveness of our sins, and rose from the dead was for the sole purpose of giving us life. Even if you already have a relationship with Jesus Christ; and have trusted him as your Savior, but you are not living life to its fullest, you can. He has more for you. I know because that's exactly the boat I found myself drifting in, but He changed all of that. He has given me a new life with eyes that see more clearly His plan for me. He has given me new joy, along with an inexpressible song in my heart. He has also given me a new day with which to express that new life and new joy.

Yes, that is the Lord, Jesus Christ that I know today. The One who came to give new life, new joy, for a new day.

He has an entirely new character from the Lord I knew before. Oh, I knew Him enough to go to heaven and live with Him some day, but that wasn't enough for me. I wanted more and He wanted more for me.

Did He change? No, "Jesus Christ is the same yesterday and today and forever." Hebrews 13:8$_{NIV}$®

But when he revealed Himself to me in such a real way, I was the one who was forever changed.

I pray that if you are that one, the one who wants to really know Jesus in all of His glorious fullness, you will be honest with Him and tell Him so. He longs for you to know Him intimately and with great passion. Don't be afraid to say, "whatever it takes, Lord," because whatever it does take for you to know Him more will be worth it all when you truly discover who He really is.

It's hard to know how to end the final chapter of this book because it is not the final chapter of my life. That won't be completed until he takes me from this life and even then, that will only be the first chapter of a new book, the one I've been longing for my whole life. Now, *that* is going to be one great story and I hope you will be one of the main characters.

References

Chapter 3

[1]"God Gave the Song," Words and music by Bill and Gloria Gaither, Copyright © 1969. All rights reserved. Used by permission.

Chapter 9

[1]"Whatever it Takes,"Words and music by Marietta E. Webster and Lanny Lavon Wolfe, Copyright © 1975 by Lanny Wolfe Music Co. % Gaither Music Publishing. All rights reserved. Used by permission.

Chapter 10

[1]"Whatever it Takes," Words and music by Marietta E. Webster and Lanny Lavon Wolfe, Copyright © 1975 by Lanny Wolfe Music Co. % Gaither Music Publishing. All rights reserved. Used by permission.

Chapter 14

[1] "Whatever it Takes," Words and music byMarietta E. Webster and Lanny Lavon Wolfe, Copyright © 1975 by Lanny Wolfe Music Co. % Gaither Music Publishing. All rights reserved. Used by permission.

About the Author

Kathy Miller has been in full-time ministry with her husband, Gary for 30 years. She has traveled, speaking and singing throughout the United States, England, Canada and Mexico. She enjoys being by Gary's side in the ministry, and loves her greatest calling of ministering to her ever-growing family. She has two children, a son-in-law, daughter-in-law and seven grandchildren(at time of publication). She is hoping for more.

Should you wish to contact Kathy for speaking engagements or for any other reason, you may reach her at:

8011 Trousdale Ferry Pike
Lebanon, TN 37090
615.417.4224
or
by e-mail
GKZMiller@charter.net